HERSHEY'S®

Make It Chocolate!

Chocolate Contents

MiniChips®
HERSHEY'S

Reese's®

Semi-Sweet Chocolate Chips
HERSHEY'S

Milk Chocolate Chips
HERSHEY'S®

HERSHEY'S
Semi-sweet
Chocolate

HERSHEY'S
ALL NATURAL
Unsweetened
Baking Chocolate

HERSHEY'S
ALL NATURAL
Unsweetened
Baking Chocolate

HERSHEY'S
Semi-swee
Chocolate

NET WT. 8 OZS. 226.8g 8 INDIVIDUALLY WRAPPED 1 OZ. BLOCKS

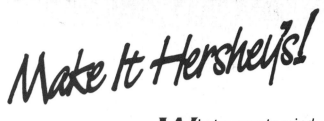

Make It Hershey's!

What comes to mind when you think about chocolate? Perhaps it's chocolate's irresistibly rich and luxurious flavor. That's why millions of us across the country are devoted chocolate lovers.

5

Milton S. Hershey was devoted to chocolate too. When Mr. Hershey made his first milk chocolate bar in 1894, little did he know that Hershey would become "America's Chocolate Authority"™.

Today, Hershey offers a rich heritage in fine quality chocolates from HERSHEY'S milk chocolate bars and HERSHEY'S KISSES® chocolates to the very best for baking with HERSHEY'S cocoa, chocolate chips, and baking chocolate. What better way to "Make It Chocolate™" than with Hershey's!

If you've made a batch of Great American Chocolate Chip Cookies from the recipe found on every bag of HERSHEY'S chocolate chips, or seen a recipe using HERSHEY'S cocoa in your favorite magazine, then you're familiar with the kind of work we do in the Hershey Kitchens. For over 30 years, we've been developing new chocolate snacks and desserts for all occasions as well as updating popular classics to fit today's lifestyles.

The Hershey's *Make It Chocolate!*™ recipe book has been designed for all chocolate-loving cooks. The key ingredient in all our recipes is chocolate, of course, and 100% pure HERSHEY'S, too. The easy-to-follow recipe instructions and special hints throughout the book help eliminate guesswork. With page after page of beautiful color photos, the Hershey's *Make It Chocolate!*™ recipe book shows you just how tempting your chocolate creations will look.

6

Photograph courtesy of John Paul Endress

Turn the pages and find popular Hershey classics and tantalizing new desserts that are quick, easy and taste like you've baked all day! From everyday family favorites and chocolate snacking treats to elegant endings and indulgent rewards, the Hershey's *Make It Chocolate!*™ recipe book will make your dessert selections easier.

If you should have any questions or comments about these recipes or any of our fine chocolate products, please write us at The Hershey Kitchens, P.O. Box 815, Hershey, PA 17033-0815, or call us toll-free, weekdays 9-4, Eastern Time, 1-800-468-1714.

The Hershey Kitchens

Everyday Family Favorites

Treat your family to this delicious buffet of everyday favorite desserts.

(Pictured: Chocolate Strawberry Shortcake, recipe page 13.)

Cocoa Marble Gingerbread

½ cup shortening
1 cup sugar
1 cup light molasses
2 eggs
1 teaspoon baking soda
1 cup boiling water
2 cups all-purpose flour
1 teaspoon salt
¼ cup HERSHEY'S Cocoa
½ teaspoon ground cinnamon
½ teaspoon ground ginger
¼ teaspoon ground nutmeg
¼ teaspoon ground cloves
 Sweetened whipped cream
 (optional)

Heat oven to 350.° Grease and flour rectangular pan, 13x9x2 inches. In large mixer bowl combine shortening, sugar and molasses; beat well. Blend in eggs. Stir baking soda into boiling water to dissolve; add alternately with flour and salt to creamed mixture. In medium bowl stir cocoa into 2 cups of batter. Add spices to remaining batter in large mixer bowl. Alternately spoon batters into prepared pan. Swirl gently with spatula. Bake 40 to 45 minutes or until wooden pick inserted in center comes out clean. Cut into squares. Serve warm or cool with sweetened whipped cream, if desired. *12 servings.*

Cocoa Applesauce Muffins

Cocoa Crunch Topping
(optional, recipe follows)
¼ cup HERSHEY'S Cocoa
¼ cup vegetable oil
¾ cup chunky applesauce
1 egg, beaten
1¼ cups all-purpose flour
¾ cup sugar
¾ teaspoon baking soda
¼ teaspoon salt
⅛ teaspoon ground cinnamon
½ cup chopped nuts

Heat oven to 400°. Grease bottoms only of 12 muffin cups (2½ inches in diameter). Prepare Cocoa Crunch Topping, if desired; set aside. In small mixing bowl combine cocoa and oil; stir until smooth. Add applesauce and egg; blend well. In medium mixing bowl combine flour, sugar, baking soda, salt and cinnamon; stir in applesauce mixture and nuts, blending just until dry ingredients are moistened. Fill muffin cups about ⅔ full. Sprinkle heaping teaspoonful topping on each muffin, if desired. Bake 25 to 30 minutes or until wooden pick inserted in center comes out clean. Let cool about 5 minutes. Remove from pan; serve warm.
About 1 dozen muffins.

Cocoa Crunch Topping

2 tablespoons butter or margarine
2 tablespoons HERSHEY'S Cocoa
2 tablespoons flour
¼ cup packed light
brown sugar
¼ cup chopped nuts
(optional)

In small bowl combine all ingredients until crumbly. (Leftover topping can be stored in covered container in refrigerator.)

11

Three-In-One Chocolate Pudding & Pie Filling

¾ cup sugar
⅓ cup **HERSHEY'S** Cocoa
2 tablespoons cornstarch
2 tablespoons all-purpose flour
¼ teaspoon salt
2 cups milk
2 egg yolks, slightly beaten
2 tablespoons butter or margarine
1 teaspoon vanilla extract

In medium saucepan combine sugar, cocoa, cornstarch, flour and salt; blend in milk and egg yolks. Cook over medium heat, stirring constantly, until mixture boils; boil and stir 1 minute. Remove from heat; blend in butter and vanilla. Pour into medium bowl or individual serving dishes; press plastic wrap directly onto surface. Cool; refrigerate. *4 servings.*

Pie: Reduce milk to 1¾ cups in recipe above; cook as directed. Pour hot pudding into 8-inch (6 ounces) packaged graham crumb crust; press plastic wrap onto surface. Chill; top with sweetened whipped cream or whipped topping before serving. *6 servings.*

Chocolate Strawberry Shortcake

Parfaits: Alternate layers of cold pudding and sweetened whipped cream or whipped topping in parfait glasses.

Microwave Directions: In 2 quart micro-proof bowl combine sugar, cocoa, cornstarch, flour and salt; blend in milk and egg yolks. Microwave on high (full power) 5 minutes, stirring several times, or until mixture boils. Microwave on high 1 to 2 additional minutes or until mixture is smooth and thickened.

6 cups fresh strawberries
¾ cup sugar, divided
1⅔ cups all-purpose flour
⅓ cup HERSHEY'S Cocoa
1 tablespoon baking powder
¼ teaspoon salt
½ cup butter or margarine
1 egg, beaten
⅔ cup milk
1 cup chilled whipping cream
2 tablespoons confectioners' sugar

Select 6 strawberries; set aside. Slice remaining berries. Combine sliced berries and ¼ cup sugar; set aside. Heat oven to 450°. Grease round pan, 8x1½ inches. In medium mixing bowl combine flour, cocoa, remaining ½ cup sugar, baking powder and salt. Cut in butter until mixture resembles coarse crumbs. Combine egg and milk; add all at once to dry ingredients and stir just to moisten. Spread dough in prepared pan, building up edges slightly. Bake 15 to 18 minutes. Cool 10 minutes. Remove from pan; place on serving plate. Beat whipping cream and confectioners' sugar until stiff. Arrange some sliced berries atop cake. Spoon whipped cream over top. Garnish with reserved whole strawberries. Serve shortcake warm with remaining sliced strawberries. *8 servings.*

Chocolate Cherry Upside-Down Cake

1 tablespoon cold water
1 tablespoon cornstarch
¼ to ½ teaspoon almond extract
　(optional)
1 can (21 ounces) cherry pie filling
1⅔ cups all-purpose flour
1 cup sugar
¼ cup HERSHEY'S Cocoa
1 teaspoon baking soda
½ teaspoon salt
1 cup water
⅓ cup vegetable oil
1 teaspoon vinegar
½ teaspoon vanilla extract

Heat oven to 350°. In medium bowl combine cold water, cornstarch and almond extract, if desired. Stir in cherry pie filling; blend well. Spread evenly on bottom of ungreased square pan, 9x9x2 inches; set aside. In medium mixing bowl combine flour, sugar, cocoa, baking soda and salt. Add water, oil, vinegar and vanilla; stir or whisk until batter is smooth and well blended. Pour evenly over cherries. Bake 40 to 45 minutes or until wooden pick inserted in center comes out clean. Cool 10 minutes; invert onto serving plate. Serve warm. *About 9 servings.*

Hot Fudge Pudding Cake

1¼ cups sugar, divided
1 cup all-purpose flour
7 tablespoons HERSHEY'S Cocoa, divided
2 teaspoons baking powder
¼ teaspoon salt
½ cup milk
⅓ cup butter or margarine, melted
1½ teaspoons vanilla extract
½ cup packed light brown sugar
1¼ cups hot water

Heat oven to 350°. In medium mixing bowl combine ¾ cup sugar, flour, 3 tablespoons cocoa, baking powder and salt. Blend in milk, melted butter and vanilla; beat until smooth. Pour batter into square pan, 8x8x2 or 9x9x2 inches. In small bowl combine remaining ½ cup sugar, brown sugar and remaining 4 tablespoons cocoa; sprinkle mixture evenly over batter. Pour hot water over top; do not stir. Bake 40 minutes or until center is almost set. Let stand 15 minutes; spoon into dessert dishes, spooning sauce from bottom of pan over top. Garnish as desired. *8 to 10 servings.*

◄Chocolate Zucchini Cake

3 eggs
1½ cups sugar
 1 teaspoon vanilla extract
 ½ cup vegetable oil
 2 cups all-purpose flour
 ⅓ cup HERSHEY'S Cocoa
 1 teaspoon baking powder
 1 teaspoon baking soda
 1 teaspoon ground cinnamon
 ¼ teaspoon salt
 ¾ cup buttermilk or sour milk*
 2 cups coarsely shredded raw
   zucchini
 1 cup chopped nuts
 ½ cup raisins
   Creamy Chocolate Chip Glaze
   (recipe follows)

Heat oven to 350° Grease and flour 12-cup Bundt pan. In large mixer bowl beat eggs well. Gradually beat in sugar and vanilla until thick and light in color. Gradually pour in oil, beating until blended. Combine flour, cocoa, baking powder, baking soda, cinnamon and salt; add alternately with buttermilk to egg mixture. Drain zucchini well; fold into batter. Stir in nuts and raisins; pour into prepared pan. Bake 55 to 60 minutes or until wooden pick inserted in center comes out clean. Cool 10 minutes; invert onto serving plate. Cool completely. Glaze with Creamy Chocolate Chip Glaze. *12 servings.*

*To sour milk: Use 2 teaspoons vinegar plus milk to equal ¾ cup.

Creamy Chocolate Chip Glaze

2 tablespoons sugar
2 tablespoons water
½ cup HERSHEY'S Semi-Sweet
    Chocolate Chips or MINI CHIPS
1 tablespoon marshmallow creme
1 to 2 teaspoons hot water

In small saucepan combine sugar and 2 tablespoons water; bring to boil. Remove from heat; immediately add chocolate chips and stir until melted. Blend in marshmallow creme; add hot water, ½ teaspoon at a time, until glaze is desired consistency. *About ½ cup glaze.*

Chocolate Frozen Yogurt

¼ cup HERSHEY'S Cocoa
¼ cup sugar
2 containers (8 ounces each)
    vanilla yogurt
¼ cup light corn syrup

In medium mixing bowl combine cocoa and sugar. Add yogurt and corn syrup; stir until well blended and smooth. Pour mixture into square pan, 8x8x2 inches or loaf pan, 9x5x3 inches. Cover; freeze several hours or overnight until firm. Spoon into large mixer bowl. With mixer on low speed, beat until smooth but not melted. Return to pan or pour into 1 pint freezer container. Cover; freeze several hours or overnight until firm. Before serving, allow to stand at room temperature about 10 minutes. *About 4 servings.*

Buried Cherry Cookies

Chocolate Frosting (recipe
  follows)
½ cup butter or margarine
1 cup sugar
1 egg
1½ teaspoons vanilla extract
1½ cups all-purpose flour
⅓ cup HERSHEY'S Cocoa
¼ teaspoon baking powder
¼ teaspoon baking soda
¼ teaspoon salt
1 jar (10 ounces) small maraschino cherries (about 44)

Prepare Chocolate Frosting; set aside.
Heat oven to 350°. In large mixer bowl
cream butter, sugar, egg and vanilla
until light and fluffy. Combine flour,
cocoa, baking powder, baking soda
and salt; gradually add to creamed
mixture until well blended. Shape
dough into 1-inch balls. Place about
2 inches apart on ungreased cookie
sheet. Press center of each cookie with
thumb to make indentation. Drain
cherries; place one cherry in center
of each cookie. Bake 10 minutes or
until edges are set. Remove from cookie
sheet; cool on wire rack. Spoon scant
teaspoonful frosting over cherry,
spreading to cover cherry.
About 3½ dozen cookies.

Chocolate Frosting

⅔ cup sweetened condensed
  milk
½ cup HERSHEY'S Semi-
  Sweet Chocolate Chips

In small saucepan combine
sweetened condensed milk
and chocolate chips. Stir constantly over low heat until
chips are melted and mixture
is smooth, about 5 minutes.
Remove from heat; cool
thoroughly.

HERSHEY'S™ Great American Chocolate Chip Cookies

1 cup butter, softened
¾ cup sugar
¾ cup packed light brown sugar
1 teaspoon vanilla extract
2 eggs
2¼ cups all-purpose flour
1 teaspoon baking soda
½ teaspoon salt
2 cups (12-ounce package)
    HERSHEY'S Semi-Sweet
    Chocolate Chips
1 cup chopped nuts (optional)

Heat oven to 375°. In large mixer bowl cream butter, sugar, brown sugar and vanilla until light and fluffy. Add eggs; beat well. Combine flour, baking soda and salt; gradually beat into creamed mixture. Stir in chocolate chips and nuts, if desired. Drop by teaspoonfuls onto ungreased cookie sheet. Bake 8 to 10 minutes or until lightly browned. Cool slightly; remove from cookie sheet onto wire rack. Cool completely. *About 6 dozen cookies.*

Pan Recipe: Spread chocolate chip batter in greased jelly-roll pan, 15½ x 10½ x 1 inch. Bake 20 minutes or until lightly browned. Cool completely; cut into bars.

SKOR & Chocolate Chips Cookies:
Use 1 cup finely chopped SKOR bars and 1 cup HERSHEY'S Semi-Sweet Chocolate Chips in place of 2 cups chocolate chips; omit nuts. Drop and bake as directed.

REESE'S™ Chewy Chocolate Cookies

1¼ cups butter or margarine,
    softened
2 cups sugar
2 eggs
2 teaspoons vanilla extract
2 cups all-purpose flour
¾ cup HERSHEY'S Cocoa
1 teaspoon baking soda
½ teaspoon salt
2 cups (12-ounce package)
    REESE'S Peanut Butter Chips

Heat oven to 350°. In large mixer bowl cream butter and sugar until light and fluffy. Add eggs and vanilla; beat well. Combine flour, cocoa, baking soda and salt; gradually blend into creamed mixture. Stir in peanut butter chips. Drop by teaspoonfuls onto ungreased cookie sheet. Bake 8 to 9 minutes. (Do not overbake; cookies will be soft. They will puff while baking and flatten while cooling.) Cool slightly; remove from cookie sheet onto wire rack. Cool completely. *About 4½ dozen cookies.*

REESE'S™ Chewy Chocolate Cookies (Top); HERSHEY'S™ Great American Chocolate Chip Cookies (Bottom).

Chocolate Quickie Stickies

6 tablespoons butter or
  margarine
¾ cup packed light brown sugar
4 tablespoons HERSHEY'S Cocoa,
  divided
5 teaspoons water
1 teaspoon vanilla extract
½ cup coarsely chopped nuts
  (optional)
2 packages (8 ounces each)
  refrigerated crescent dinner
  rolls
2½ tablespoons butter or
  margarine, softened
2 tablespoons sugar

Heat oven to 350° In small saucepan over low heat melt 6 tablespoons butter. Add brown sugar, 3 tablespoons cocoa and water. Cook over medium heat, stirring constantly, just until mixture comes to boil. Remove from heat; add vanilla. Spoon about 1 teaspoonful chocolate mixture into each of 48 small muffin pans (1¾ inches in diameter). Sprinkle ½ teaspoon nuts, if desired, into each cup; set aside. Separate rolls into 8 rectangles; firmly press diagonal perforations to seal. Combine softened butter, sugar and remaining 1 tablespoon cocoa; evenly spread thin layer over each rectangle. Starting at longer side, roll up. Pinch seams to seal. Cut each roll into 6 equal pieces. Place in prepared pans, cut side down. Bake 11 to 13 minutes or until light brown. Remove from oven; cool 30 seconds. Invert onto cookie sheet. Let stand 1 minute; remove pan. Serve warm or cool. *4 dozen small rolls.*

Note: Rolls can be baked in 2 round pans, 8 x 1½ inches. Heat oven to 350° Cook chocolate mixture as directed; place ½ in each pan. Prepare rolls as directed; place 24 pieces, cut side down, in each pan. Bake 20 to 22 minutes. Cool and remove from pan, as above.

Fudge Caramels

2 cups sugar
⅔ cup HERSHEY'S Cocoa
⅛ teaspoon salt
1 cup light corn syrup
1 cup evaporated milk
½ cup water
¼ cup butter
1 teaspoon vanilla extract

Butter square pan, 9 x 9 x 2 inches; set aside. In heavy 3-quart saucepan combine sugar, cocoa, salt and corn syrup; add evaporated milk and water. Cook over medium heat, stirring constantly, until mixture boils. Cook, stirring frequently, to 245°F (firm-ball stage) or until syrup, when dropped into very cold water, forms a firm ball that does not flatten when removed from water. Remove from heat; stir in butter and vanilla, blending well. Pour into prepared pan. Cool; with buttered scissors cut into 1-inch squares. Wrap individually. *About 6 dozen candies.*

Chocolate Quickie Stickies; Fudge Caramels; Mint Frosted Brownies.

Mint Frosted Brownies

2 eggs
1 cup sugar
½ cup butter or margarine, melted
1 teaspoon vanilla extract
⅔ cup all-purpose flour
6 tablespoons HERSHEY'S Cocoa
½ teaspoon baking powder
¼ teaspoon salt
½ cup chopped walnuts (optional)
    Mint Frosting (recipe follows)

Heat oven to 350°. Grease square pan, 8x8x2 inches. In small mixer bowl beat eggs well; gradually beat in sugar. Blend in melted butter and vanilla. Combine flour, cocoa, baking powder and salt; add to egg mixture, blending thoroughly. Stir in nuts, if desired. Spread batter into prepared pan. Bake 20 to 25 minutes or just until brownies begin to pull away from sides of pan. Cook; frost with Mint Frosting. Cut into squares when frosting is set.
16 brownies.

Mint Frosting

2 tablespoons butter or
    margarine, softened
1 cup confectioners' sugar
1 to 2 tablespoons milk
¼ teaspoon vanilla extract
⅛ teaspoon mint extract
3 to 4 drops green or red food color

In small mixer bowl combine all ingredients; beat until creamy and desired consistency.

21

Banana Split Pie

Crumb-Nut Crust (recipe
    follows)
1¼ cups sugar
⅓ cup cornstarch
⅓ cup HERSHEY'S Cocoa
¼ teaspoon salt
2½ cups milk
2 egg yolks, slightly beaten
3 tablespoons butter or
    margarine
1 teaspoon vanilla extract
2 medium bananas, sliced
Frozen whipped topping,
    thawed
Chopped peanuts
Additional banana slices
Maraschino cherries

Prepare and bake Crumb-Nut Crust; cool. In medium saucepan stir together sugar, cornstarch, cocoa and salt. Blend milk and egg yolks; gradually stir into sugar mixture. Cook over medium heat, stirring constantly, until mixture thickens and boils. Boil and stir over low heat 3 minutes. Remove from heat, blend in butter and vanilla. Press plastic wrap directly onto filling; cool about 20 minutes. Arrange banana slices over bottom of crust. Pour filling over bananas; press plastic wrap onto filling. Refrigerate 3 to 4 hours. Remove plastic wrap; top pie with dollops of whipped topping. Garnish with chopped peanuts, banana slices and maraschino cherries. *8 servings.*

Crumb-Nut Crust

1¼ cups graham cracker crumbs
¼ cup finely chopped peanuts
⅓ cup butter or margarine, melted

Heat oven to 350°. In medium bowl combine all ingredients; press evenly on bottom and up sides of 9-inch pie plate. Bake 8 to 10 minutes.

Chocolatetown Pie

9-inch unbaked pastry shell
½ cup butter or margarine,
   softened
2 eggs, beaten
2 teaspoons vanilla extract or 2
   tablespoons bourbon
1 cup sugar
⅓ cup all-purpose flour
1 cup HERSHEY'S Semi-Sweet
   Chocolate Chips or MINI CHIPS
1 cup chopped pecans or walnuts
   Festive Whipped Cream
   (optional, recipe follows)

Prepare pastry shell; set aside. Heat oven to 350° In small mixer bowl cream butter; add eggs and vanilla or bourbon. Combine sugar and flour; add to creamed mixture. Stir in chocolate chips and nuts; pour into unbaked pastry shell. Bake 45 to 50 minutes or until golden. Cool about one hour; serve warm. Garnish with Festive Whipped Cream, if desired. *8 to 10 servings.*

FESTIVE WHIPPED CREAM
In small mixer bowl combine ½ cup chilled whipping cream, 2 tablespoons confectioners' sugar and ¼ teaspoon vanilla extract or 1 teaspoon bourbon; beat until stiff. *About 1 cup topping.*

23

Old-Fashioned Chocolate Cake

¾ cup butter or margarine
1⅔ cups sugar
3 eggs
1 teaspoon vanilla extract
2 cups all-purpose flour
⅔ cup HERSHEY'S Cocoa
1¼ teaspoons baking soda
¼ teaspoon baking powder
1 teaspoon salt
1⅓ cups water
½ cup finely crushed hard
    peppermint candy (optional)
One-Bowl Buttercream Frosting
    (recipe page 72)

Heat oven to 350° Grease and flour 2 round pans, 9x1½ inches or rectangular pan, 13x9x2 inches. In large mixer bowl combine butter, sugar, eggs and vanilla. Beat on high speed 3 minutes. Combine flour, cocoa, baking soda, baking powder and salt; add alternately with water to creamed mixture. Blend just until combined; add candy, if desired. Pour into prepared pan(s). Bake 30 to 35 minutes or until wooden pick inserted in center comes out clean. Cool 10 minutes; remove from pan(s). Cool completely; frost with One-Bowl Buttercream Frosting. *8 to 10 servings.*

Chocolate Cupcakes: Fill paper-lined muffin cups (2½ inches in diameter) ⅔ full with batter. Bake at 350° for 20 to 25 minutes. Cool; frost. *About 2½ dozen cupcakes.*

Mississippi Mud Cake

½ cup butter or margarine
1 cup sugar
1 teaspoon vanilla extract
3 eggs
¾ cup all-purpose flour
⅓ cup HERSHEY'S Cocoa
½ teaspoon baking powder
  Dash salt
1 cup chopped pecans
1 package (10½ ounces) miniature
  marshmallows
  One-Bowl Buttercream Frosting
  (recipe page 72)

Heat oven to 350°. Grease rectangular pan, 13x9x2 inches. In large mixer bowl cream butter, sugar and vanilla until light and fluffy. Add eggs, one at a time, beating well after each addition. Combine flour, cocoa, baking powder and salt; add to creamed mixture. Stir in nuts. Spoon batter into prepared pan. Bake 15 to 18 minutes or until top is barely soft to the touch. Meanwhile, prepare frosting. Remove cake from oven; immediately cover top with marshmallows. Return cake to oven 2 to 3 minutes or until marshmallows are soft. Gently spread marshmallows over cake; immediately spread frosting over top. Cool thoroughly before cutting cake into squares.
12 to 15 servings.

Chocolate Snacking Treats

Create a delicious variety of tantalizing munchies and assorted fun finger foods for school lunch boxes, cookie jars, picnics or after school snacks.

(Pictured: Five Layer Bars, recipe page 36; Cocoa Cherry Drops, recipe page 28.)

Cocoa Cherry Drops

½ cup plus 2 tablespoons butter
   or margarine
1 cup sugar
1 egg
1 teaspoon vanilla extract
1¼ cups all-purpose flour
6 tablespoons HERSHEY'S Cocoa
½ teaspoon baking soda
½ teaspoon salt
1 cup chopped maraschino
   cherries, well drained
½ cup chopped walnuts
   Walnut pieces (optional)

Heat oven to 350°. In large mixer bowl
cream butter and sugar. Add egg and
vanilla; blend well. Combine flour,
cocoa, baking soda and salt; blend into
creamed mixture. Stir in cherries and
nuts. Drop by rounded teaspoonfuls
onto ungreased cookie sheet. Press
walnut piece into each cookie, if
desired. Bake 10 to 12 minutes or
until set. Cool slightly; remove from
cookie sheet. Cool on wire rack.
About 4 dozen cookies.

▼Cut Out Chocolate Cookies

½ cup butter or margarine
¾ cup sugar
1 egg
1 teaspoon vanilla extract
1½ cups all-purpose flour
⅓ cup HERSHEY'S Cocoa
½ teaspoon baking powder
½ teaspoon baking soda
¼ teaspoon salt
Satiny Chocolate Glaze
   (recipe follows)
Vanilla Glaze (recipe follows)

In large mixer bowl cream butter,
sugar, egg and vanilla until light and
fluffy. Combine flour, cocoa, baking
powder, baking soda and salt; add to
creamed mixture, blending well. Chill
dough about 1 hour or until firm
enough to roll. Heat oven to 325°. Roll
small portion of dough at a time on
lightly floured board or between 2
pieces of wax paper to ¼-inch
thickness. Cut into desired shapes with
cookie cutters; place on ungreased
cookie sheet. Bake 5 to 7 minutes or
until no indentation remains when
touched lightly. Cool slightly; remove
from cookie sheet. Cool on wire rack.
Frost with Satiny Chocolate Glaze or
Vanilla Glaze. *About 3 dozen cookies.*

Vanilla Glaze

3 tablespoons butter or margarine
2 cups confectioners' sugar
1 teaspoon vanilla extract
2 to 3 tablespoons milk
2 to 4 drops food color (optional)

In small saucepan over low heat melt butter. Remove from heat; blend in confectioners' sugar and vanilla. Add milk gradually; beat until desired consistency. Blend in food color, if desired. *About 1 cup glaze.*

Satiny Chocolate Glaze

2 tablespoons butter or margarine
3 tablespoons HERSHEY'S Cocoa
2 tablespoons water
1 cup confectioners' sugar
½ teaspoon vanilla extract

In small saucepan over low heat melt butter; add cocoa and water, stirring constantly until mixture thickens. Do not boil. Remove from heat; gradually add confectioners' sugar and vanilla, beating with whisk until smooth. Add additional water, ½ teaspoon at a time, until desired consistency. *About ¾ cup glaze.*

▲ Chocolate Crinkle Cookies

2 cups sugar
¾ cup vegetable oil
¾ cup HERSHEY'S Cocoa
4 eggs
2 teaspoons vanilla extract
2⅓ cups all-purpose flour
2 teaspoons baking powder
½ teaspoon salt
    Confectioners' sugar

In large mixer bowl combine sugar and oil. Add cocoa; blend well. Beat in eggs and vanilla. Combine flour, baking powder and salt; add to cocoa mixture, blending well. Cover; chill at least 6 hours. Heat oven to 350.° Shape dough into 1-inch balls. Roll in confectioners' sugar. Place 2 inches apart on greased cookie sheet. Bake 12 to 14 minutes or until almost no indentation remains when touched. Remove from cookie sheet; cool on wire rack.
About 4 dozen cookies.

Chewy Chocolate Macaroons

1 package (14 ounces) flaked
    coconut (about 5⅓ cups)
½ cup HERSHEY'S Cocoa
1 can (14 ounces) sweetened
    condensed milk
2 teaspoons vanilla extract
    Red candied cherries, halved

Heat oven to 350.° In large mixing bowl thoroughly combine coconut and cocoa; stir in sweetened condensed milk and vanilla. Drop by rounded teaspoonfuls onto generously greased cookie sheet. Press cherry half into each cookie. Bake 8 to 10 minutes or until almost set. Immediately remove from cookie sheet onto wire rack; cool completely. Store loosely covered at room temperature.
About 4 dozen cookies.

Peanutty-Cocoa Bonbons

2 packages (3 ounces each) cream
   cheese, softened
1 tablespoon milk
4 cups confectioners' sugar
1/3 cup HERSHEY'S Cocoa
1 teaspoon vanilla extract
1 cup finely chopped nuts
   (optional)
2 cups (12-ounce package)
   REESE'S Peanut Butter Chips
2 tablespoons shortening (not
   butter, margarine or oil)

In large mixer bowl beat cream cheese
and milk until fluffy. Blend in confectioners' sugar, cocoa and vanilla. Stir
in nuts, if desired. Cover; chill several
hours or until firm enough to handle.
To form centers shape into ¾-inch
balls. Place on wax paper-lined tray.
Refrigerate, uncovered, 3 to 4 hours
or until dry.

To coat: In top of double boiler over
hot, not boiling, water melt peanut
butter chips and shortening, stirring
constantly to blend. Set aside; cool
slightly. Dip chilled centers into peanut
butter mixture; remove with fork.
(To remove excess coating, slide fork
across rim of pan and tap a few times.)
Slide from fork onto wax paper, swirling "thread" of peanut butter across
top for decoration. (If coating becomes
too thick, reheat over hot water.)
Refrigerate bonbons, uncovered,
1 hour. Store in cool, dry place.
About 10 dozen bonbons.

Microwave Directions: Make centers
as directed. For coating: In 1-quart
micro-proof bowl place peanut
butter chips and shortening.
Microwave on high (full power)
1 to 2 minutes, stirring once, or
just until chips are melted and
mixture is smooth when stirred.
Coat and store as directed.

Apple-Chip Snacking Cake

2 eggs
½ cup vegetable oil
¼ cup bottled apple juice
1 teaspoon vanilla extract
1¾ cups all-purpose flour
1 cup sugar
½ teaspoon baking soda
½ teaspoon ground cinnamon
½ teaspoon salt
1½ cups diced peeled tart apples
¾ cup HERSHEY'S Semi-Sweet
    Chocolate Chips or
    MINI CHIPS
½ cup chopped nuts
    Confectioners' sugar or
    whipped topping and
    cinnamon (optional)

Heat oven to 350.° Grease and flour square pan, 9x9x2 inches. In large mixing bowl beat eggs slightly; add oil, apple juice and vanilla. Combine flour, sugar, baking soda, cinnamon and salt; stir into batter until combined. Add apples, chocolate chips and nuts; stir until well blended. Pour into prepared pan. Bake 40 to 45 minutes or until cake begins to pull away from sides of pan. Cool completely. Sprinkle top with confectioners' sugar or serve with dollop of whipped topping sprinkled with cinnamon, if desired. *9 servings*.

Cocoa-Cola Cake

2 cups sugar
2 cups all-purpose flour
½ cup vegetable oil
½ cup butter or margarine
⅓ cup HERSHEY'S Cocoa
1 cup cola (not diet)
1½ cups miniature marshmallows
½ cup buttermilk or sour milk*
1 teaspoon baking soda
2 eggs, slightly beaten
1 teaspoon vanilla extract
    Chocolate Nut Frosting
    (recipe follows)

Heat oven to 350° Grease rectangular pan, 13x9x2 inches. In large mixer bowl combine sugar and flour; set aside. In medium saucepan combine oil, butter, cocoa and cola. Bring to boil over medium heat, stirring constantly. Add chocolate mixture to sugar mixture; beat until smooth. Stir in marshmallows. Add buttermilk, baking soda, eggs and vanilla; blend well. Pour into prepared pan. Bake 40 to 45 minutes or until wooden pick inserted in center comes out clean. Meanwhile, prepare Chocolate Nut Frosting; spread over warm cake. Cool completely.
12 to 15 servings.

*To sour milk: Use 1½ teaspoons vinegar plus milk to equal ½ cup.

Chocolate Nut Frosting

3⅔ cups (1 pound) confectioners'
    sugar
½ cup butter or margarine
6 tablespoons cola (not diet)
3 tablespoons HERSHEY'S Cocoa
½ to 1 cup coarsely chopped
    pecans
1 teaspoon vanilla extract

In small mixer bowl place confectioners' sugar; set aside. In small saucepan combine butter, cola and cocoa. Bring to boil over medium heat, stirring constantly. Pour hot mixture over confectioners' sugar; beat until smooth and slightly thickened. Stir in pecans and vanilla.
About 2½ cups frosting.

Cocoa Spice Snacking Cake

¼ cup butter or margarine, melted
¼ cup HERSHEY'S Cocoa
¾ cup applesauce
1 cup all-purpose flour
1 cup sugar
¾ teaspoon baking soda
½ teaspoon ground cinnamon
¼ teaspoon ground nutmeg
¼ teaspoon salt
1 egg, slightly beaten
½ cup chopped nuts
½ cup raisins
    Confectioners' sugar (optional)

Heat oven to 350° Grease square pan, 9x9x2 inches. In small mixing bowl combine melted butter and cocoa, stirring until smooth; blend in applesauce. In large mixing bowl combine flour, sugar, baking soda, cinnamon, nutmeg and salt. Add cocoa mixture and egg; stir until dry ingredients are moistened. Stir in nuts and raisins. Spread into prepared pan; bake 30 to 35 minutes or until wooden pick inserted into center comes out clean. Cool in pan. Cut into squares. Sprinkle top with confectioners' sugar, if desired.
9 servings.

Double Decker Fudge

2 cups (12-ounce package)
   REESE'S Peanut Butter Chips,
   divided
¼ cup butter, melted
½ cup HERSHEY'S Cocoa
1 teaspoon vanilla extract
4½ cups sugar
1 jar (7 ounces) marshmallow
   creme
1½ cups (12-ounce can)
   evaporated milk
¼ cup butter

1. Line rectangular pan, 13x9x2
   inches, with aluminum foil. In
   medium mixing bowl place 1 cup
   peanut butter chips; set aside.
   In second medium mixing bowl,
   blend melted butter, cocoa and
   vanilla until smooth; add 1 cup
   peanut butter chips.

2. In heavy 4-quart saucepan combine sugar, marshmallow creme,
   evaporated milk and butter. Cook,
   stirring constantly, over medium
   heat until mixture comes to rolling
   boil; boil and stir 5 minutes.

3. Remove from heat. Immediately
   add half of hot mixture to bowl
   with peanut butter chips only. Pour
   remainder into cocoa mixture; stir
   to blend.

4. Beat peanut butter mixture until
   chips are completely melted; spread
   evenly in prepared pan.

5. Beat cocoa mixture until chips
   are melted and mixture thickens.
   Spread evenly over top of peanut
   butter layer.

6. Cool until set. Remove foil; cut into
   squares. Store in airtight container
   in cool, dry place.
   About 8 dozen squares.

▲ Cocoa Party Mix

3 cups toasted oat cereal rings
3 cups bite-size crispy wheat
    squares cereal
2 cups salted peanuts
2 cups miniature pretzels
1 cup raisins
½ cup butter or margarine, melted
2 to 4 tablespoons HERSHEY'S
    Cocoa
¼ cup sugar

Heat oven to 250°. In large mixing bowl combine cereals, peanuts, pretzels and raisins. In small mixing bowl blend melted butter, cocoa and sugar; stir into cereal mixture. Toss until ingredients are well coated. Pour mixture into rectangular pan, 13x9x2 inches. Bake 1 hour, stirring every 15 minutes. Cool completely. Store in airtight container. *About 10 cups mix.*

Cocoa Crispy Treats

6 tablespoons butter or margarine
¼ cup peanut butter
1 package (10 ounces) regular
    marshmallows (about 40) or 4
    cups miniature marshmallows
⅓ cup HERSHEY'S Cocoa
4 cups crisped rice cereal
½ cup unsalted peanuts or REESE'S
    Peanut Butter Chips or
    HERSHEY'S Semi-Sweet
    Chocolate Chips

Butter square pan, 9x9x2 inches. In large saucepan over low heat melt butter and peanut butter. Add marshmallows and stir until completely melted and well blended. Remove from heat. Stir in cocoa; blend well. Add cereal and peanuts. Stir until cereal is well coated. Using buttered spatula or wax paper, press mixture evenly into prepared pan. Cool completely; cut into squares. *About 16 squares.*

Five Layer Bars

¾ cup butter or margarine
1¾ cups graham cracker crumbs
¼ cup HERSHEY'S Cocoa
2 tablespoons sugar
1 can (14 ounces) sweetened
  condensed milk
1 cup HERSHEY'S Semi-Sweet
  Chocolate Chips
1 cup raisins or chopped dried
  apricots or miniature
  marshmallows
1 cup chopped nuts

Heat oven to 350°. In rectangular pan, 13x9x2 inches, melt butter in oven. Combine crumbs, cocoa and sugar; sprinkle over butter. Pour sweetened condensed milk evenly over crumbs. Sprinkle with chocolate chips and raisins. Sprinkle nuts on top; press down firmly. Bake 25 to 30 minutes or until lightly browned. Cool completely; cover with aluminum foil. Let stand at room temperature about 8 hours before cutting into bars.
About 3 dozen bars.

Golden Bars: Substitute 1 cup REESE'S Peanut Butter Chips for chocolate chips. Sprinkle 1 cup golden raisins or chopped dried apricots over chips. Proceed as above.

▼Chocolate Fruit Bars

2 cups vanilla wafer crumbs
½ cup HERSHEY'S Cocoa
3 tablespoons sugar
⅔ cup butter or margarine
1 cup REESE'S Peanut Butter Chips
½ cup chopped dates
½ cup red candied cherries, halved
½ cup green candied cherries,
  halved
1 can (14 ounces) sweetened
  condensed milk
¾ cup coarsely broken pecans

Heat oven to 350°. In medium mixing bowl combine crumbs, cocoa and sugar; with pastry blender blend in butter until well combined. Press mixture on bottom and ½ inch up sides of rectangular pan, 13x9x2 inches. Sprinkle peanut butter chips, then dates and cherries over crust. Pour sweetened condensed milk evenly over fruit. Sprinkle nuts on top; press down lightly. Bake 25 to 30 minutes or until edges of filling are lightly browned and center is bubbly. Cool completely; cover with aluminum foil. Let stand at room temperature about 8 hours before cutting into bars.
About 3 dozen bars.

▼Chocolate Filled Walnut-Oatmeal Bars

1 cup butter or margarine
2 cups packed light brown sugar
2 eggs
1 teaspoon vanilla extract
½ teaspoon powdered instant
   coffee (optional)
3 cups quick-cooking oats
2½ cups all-purpose flour
1 teaspoon baking soda
½ teaspoon salt
1½ cups chopped walnuts, divided
   Chocolate Filling (recipe follows)

Heat oven to 350°. In large mixer bowl cream butter and brown sugar until light and fluffy. Add eggs, vanilla and instant coffee, if desired; beat well. Combine oats, flour, baking soda, salt and 1 cup walnuts; gradually add to creamed mixture. (Batter will be stiff; stir in last part by hand.) Remove 2 cups dough; set aside. Press remaining dough evenly over bottom of jelly-roll pan, 15½ x 10½ x 1 inch. Prepare Chocolate Filling. Spread filling evenly over oatmeal mixture in pan. Sprinkle remaining oatmeal mixture over chocolate. Sprinkle remaining ½ cup nuts over top. Bake 25 minutes or until top is golden (chocolate will be soft). Cool completely; cut into bars.
About 4 dozen bars

Chocolate Filling

½ cup butter or margarine
⅔ cup HERSHEY'S Cocoa
½ cup sugar
1 can (14 ounces) sweetened
   condensed milk
1½ teaspoons vanilla extract

In medium saucepan over low heat melt butter. Stir in cocoa and sugar. Add sweetened condensed milk; cook, stirring constantly, until smooth and thick. Remove from heat. Stir in vanilla.

▼ Marbled Brownies

Nut Cream Filling (recipe page 39)
½ cup butter or margarine
⅓ cup HERSHEY'S Cocoa
2 eggs
1 cup sugar
1 teaspoon vanilla extract
½ cup all-purpose flour
½ teaspoon baking powder
¼ teaspoon salt

Prepare Nut Cream Filling; set aside.
Heat oven to 350°. Grease square pan,
9x9x2 inches. In small saucepan melt
butter; remove from heat. Stir in cocoa,
blending well. Set aside; cool slightly.
In small mixer bowl beat eggs until
foamy. Gradually add sugar and
vanilla; blend well. Combine flour,
baking powder and salt; blend into
egg mixture. Stir in chocolate mixture.
Remove ¾ cup batter; set aside.
Spread remaining batter into prepared pan. Spread Nut Cream Filling
over chocolate. Drop teaspoonfuls
of reserved chocolate over top. Use
metal spatula to swirl top chocolate
batter into nut cream layer. Bake
35 to 40 minutes or until brownies
begin to pull away from sides of pan.
Cool completely; cut into squares.
About 20 brownies.

Nut Cream Filling

1 package (3 ounces) cream
  cheese, softened
2 tablespoons butter or margarine
1/4 cup sugar
1 egg
1/2 teaspoon vanilla extract
1/4 to 1/2 teaspoon almond extract
1 tablespoon all-purpose flour
1/4 cup slivered almonds, toasted
  and chopped*

In small mixer bowl combine cream
cheese, butter and sugar; beat until
creamy. Blend in egg, vanilla and
almond extract. Stir in flour and
almonds.

*To toast almonds: On cookie sheet
spread almonds. Bake at 350°, stirring
occasionally, until lightly browned,
about 8 to 10 minutes.

1/3 cup butter or margarine
1/2 cup sugar
1/3 cup honey
2 teaspoons vanilla extract
2 eggs
1/2 cup all-purpose flour
1/3 cup HERSHEY'S Cocoa
1/2 teaspoon salt
2/3 cup chopped nuts
  Creamy Brownie Frosting
    (optional, recipe page 67)

Heat oven to 350°. Grease square pan,
9x9x2 inches. In small mixer bowl
cream butter and sugar; blend in honey
and vanilla. Add eggs; beat well.
Combine flour, cocoa and salt; gradually add to creamed mixture. Stir in
nuts. Spread into prepared pan. Bake
25 to 30 minutes or until brownies
begin to pull away from sides of pan.
Cool in pan; frost with Creamy Brownie
Frosting, if desired. Cut into squares.
About 16 brownies.

Chocolate & Company

Make it chocolate and make it special with these elegant desserts for company and holiday entertaining.

(Pictured: HERSHEY'S Chocolate Peppermint Log, recipe page 42.)

HERSHEY'S Chocolate Peppermint Log

4 eggs, separated
½ cup sugar
1 teaspoon vanilla extract
⅓ cup sugar
⅓ cup HERSHEY'S Cocoa
½ cup all-purpose flour
½ teaspoon baking powder
¼ teaspoon baking soda
⅛ teaspoon salt
⅓ cup water
    Peppermint Filling (recipe
      follows)
    Chocolate Glaze (recipe follows)

Heat oven to 375°. Line jelly-roll pan, 15½x10½x1 inch, with aluminum foil; generously grease foil. In large mixer bowl beat egg whites until foamy; gradually add ½ cup sugar, beating until stiff peaks form. Set aside. In small mixer bowl beat egg yolks and vanilla on high speed about 3 minutes; gradually add ⅓ cup sugar. Continue beating 2 additional minutes. Combine dry ingredients; add to egg yolk mixture alternately with water on low speed, beating just until batter is smooth. Gradually fold chocolate mixture into egg whites; spread evenly in prepared pan. Bake 12 to 15 minutes or until top springs back when touched lightly in center. Immediately loosen cake from edges of pan; invert on towel sprinkled with confectioners' sugar. Carefully remove foil. Immediately roll cake in towel starting from narrow end; place on wire rack to cool. Prepare Peppermint Filling. Unroll cake; remove towel. Spread with filling; reroll cake. Glaze with Chocolate Glaze; chill. *10 to 12 servings.*

PEPPERMINT FILLING

In small mixer bowl beat 1 cup chilled whipping cream until slightly thickened. Add ¼ cup confectioners' sugar and ¼ cup finely crushed peppermint candy or ½ teaspoon mint extract and a few drops red food color, if desired; beat until stiff.

Chocolate Glaze

2 tablespoons butter or margarine
2 tablespoons HERSHEY'S Cocoa
2 tablespoons water
1 cup confectioners' sugar
½ teaspoon vanilla extract

In small saucepan over low heat melt butter; add cocoa and water, stirring until smooth and slightly thickened. Do not boil. Remove from heat; cool slightly. (Cool completely for thicker, frosting-type topping.) Gradually blend in confectioners' sugar and vanilla. *About ¾ cup glaze.*

To Roll Cake: Loosen cake from edges of pan; invert on towel sprinkled with confectioners' sugar. Carefully remove foil. Immediately roll cake in towel starting from narrow end; place on wire rack to cool.

Mocha Cheesecake

Chocolate Cookie Crust
  (recipe follows)
4 packages (3 ounces each)
  cream cheese, softened
2½ tablespoons butter or
  margarine, softened
1 cup sugar
2 eggs
5 tablespoons HERSHEY'S Cocoa
¾ teaspoon vanilla extract
1 tablespoon powdered
  instant coffee
1 teaspoon boiling water
1 cup dairy sour cream

Prepare Chocolate Cookie Crust; set aside. Heat oven to 325.° In large mixer bowl beat cream cheese and butter until smooth and fluffy. Gradually beat in sugar. Add eggs, one at a time, beating well after each addition. Beat in cocoa and vanilla. Dissolve instant coffee in water; stir into cheese mixture. Add sour cream; blend well. Pour into pan. Bake 30 minutes. Turn off oven; leave cheesecake in oven 15 minutes without opening door. Remove from oven. Cool completely; cover and refrigerate. Garnish as desired.
10 to 12 servings.

Chocolate Cookie Crust

22 chocolate wafers (½ of 8½
  ounce package)
¼ cup cold butter or margarine,
  cut into ½ inch slices
⅛ teaspoon ground cinnamon

Crush wafers in food processor or blender to form fine crumbs. In medium bowl mix crumbs, butter and cinnamon until evenly blended. Press mixture evenly on bottom of 9-inch springform pan

43

German Chocolate Cake

¼ cup HERSHEY'S Cocoa
½ cup boiling water
1 cup plus 3 tablespoons butter
   or margarine
2¼ cups sugar
1 teaspoon vanilla extract
4 eggs
2 cups all-purpose flour
1 teaspoon baking soda
½ teaspoon salt
1 cup buttermilk or sour milk*
   Coconut Pecan Frosting (recipe
   follows)
   Pecan halves (optional)

In small bowl combine cocoa and water; stir until smooth. Set aside to cool. Heat oven to 350°. Grease 3 round pans, 9 x 1½ inches; line bottoms with wax paper. In large mixer bowl cream butter. Add sugar and vanilla; beat until light and fluffy. Add eggs, one at a time, beating well after each addition. Combine flour, baking soda and salt; add alternately with chocolate mixture and buttermilk to creamed mixture. Mix only until smooth. Pour batter into prepared pans. Bake 25 to 30 minutes or until top springs back when touched lightly in center. Cool 5 minutes; remove from pans and peel off paper. Cool completely. Prepare Coconut Pecan Frosting. Spread frosting between layers and over top. Garnish with pecan halves, if desired. *10 to 12 servings.*

*To sour milk: Use 1 tablespoon vinegar plus milk to equal 1 cup.

Coconut Pecan Frosting

1 can (14-ounces) sweetened
   condensed milk
3 egg yolks, beaten
½ cup butter or margarine
1 teaspoon vanilla extract
1 can (3½ ounces) flaked coconut
   (about 1⅓ cups)
1 cup chopped pecans

In heavy 2-quart saucepan combine sweetened condensed milk, egg yolks and butter. Cook, stirring constantly, over medium heat until mixture is thickened and bubbly, about 10 minutes. Remove from heat and stir in vanilla, coconut and pecans. Cool about 15 minutes.
About 2¾ cups frosting.

44

HERSHEY'S Chocolate Fudge Cake

¾ cup butter or margarine
1⅔ cups sugar
3 eggs
1½ teaspoons vanilla extract
2 cups all-purpose flour
⅔ cup HERSHEY'S Cocoa
1¼ teaspoons baking soda
½ teaspoon baking powder
½ teaspoon salt
1⅓ cups milk
    Chocolate Fudge Frosting
    (recipe follows)

Heat oven to 350°. Grease and flour 2 round pans, 9x1½ inches or rectangular pan, 13x9x2 inches. In large mixer bowl cream butter; add sugar gradually and continue beating until light and fluffy. Add eggs, one at a time, beating well after each addition. Blend in vanilla. Beat at medium speed 5 minutes, scraping sides of bowl occasionally. Combine flour, cocoa, baking soda, baking powder and salt; add to creamed mixture alternately with milk, beginning and ending with dry ingredients and beating only enough to blend. Pour batter into prepared pan(s). Bake 35 to 40 minutes or until wooden pick inserted in center comes out clean. Cool cake in rounds 10 minutes. Remove from pans; cool completely. (Do not remove cake from rectangular pan.) Frost with Chocolate Fudge Frosting. *8 to 10 servings.*

Chocolate Fudge Frosting*

¾ cup butter or margarine
1 cup HERSHEY'S Cocoa
4 cups confectioners' sugar
½ cup hot milk
2 teaspoons vanilla extract

In small saucepan over low heat melt butter; add cocoa, stirring constantly until smooth and slightly thickened. Remove from heat; set aside to cool slightly. In large mixer bowl combine confectioners' sugar and milk; beat until smooth. Add chocolate mixture and vanilla. Beat on medium speed until smooth and slightly thickened, about 5 to 10 minutes. Cool at room temperature to spreading consistency, about ½ hour. *About 3 cups frosting.*

*For 13x9x2 inch cake use 6 tablespoons butter or margarine, ½ cup cocoa, 2 cups confectioners' sugar, ¼ cup hot milk and 1 teaspoon vanilla extract; follow directions above for preparation. *About 1½ cups frosting.*

Cocoa Chiffon Cake

2 cups sugar, divided
1½ cups cake flour
⅔ cup HERSHEY'S Cocoa
2 teaspoons baking powder
1 teaspoon salt
½ teaspoon baking soda
½ cup vegetable oil
7 eggs, separated and at room
   temperature
¾ cup cold water
2 teaspoons vanilla extract
½ teaspoon cream of tartar
   Vanilla Glaze (recipe follows)

Heat oven to 325.° In large mixing bowl combine 1¾ cups sugar, flour, cocoa, baking powder, salt and baking soda. Add oil, egg yolks, water and vanilla; beat until smooth. In large mixer bowl beat egg whites and cream of tartar until foamy. Gradually add remaining ¼ cup sugar and beat until stiff peaks form. Gradually pour chocolate batter over beaten egg whites, folding with rubber spatula just until blended. Pour into ungreased 10-inch tube pan. Bake 1 hour and 20 minutes or until top springs back when touched lightly. Invert pan on heatproof funnel until completely cool. Remove cake from pan; invert onto serving plate. Spread top of cake with Vanilla Glaze, allowing some to drizzle down side. *12 to 16 servings.*

Vanilla Glaze

⅓ cup butter or margarine
2 cups confectioners' sugar
1½ teaspoons vanilla extract
2 to 4 tablespoons hot water

In medium saucepan over low heat melt butter. Remove from heat. Stir in confectioners' sugar and vanilla. Stir in water, 1 tablespoon at a time, until smooth and of desired consistency. *About 1¼ cups glaze.*

Chocolate Dipped Fruit ▶

**1 cup HERSHEY'S Semi-Sweet
   Chocolate Chips
1 tablespoon shortening
   (not butter, margarine or oil)
   Assorted fresh fruit, washed and
   chilled**

In top of double boiler over hot, not
boiling, water melt chocolate chips
and shortening; stir until smooth. Allow
mixture to cool slightly. Dip fruit or fruit
slices about ⅔ of the way into chocolate mixture. Shake gently to remove
excess chocolate. Place on wax paper-
covered tray. Refrigerate, uncovered,
until chocolate is firm, about 30 minutes. *About ½ cup coating.*

Microwave Directions: In small
micro-proof bowl melt chocolate chips
and shortening on high (full power) 1
to 1½ minutes or just until chips are
melted and mixture is smooth when
stirred. Allow to cool slightly. Dip and
serve fruit as directed above.

Fruited Chocolate Sorbet

**1 medium-size ripe banana
1½ cups orange juice
   ½ cup sugar
   ¼ cup HERSHEY'S Cocoa
1 cup chilled whipping cream**

Slice banana into blender container.
Add orange juice; blend until smooth.
Add sugar and cocoa; blend until
thoroughly combined. Add whipping
cream; blend well. Pour mixture into
square pan, 9x9x2 inches or two ice
cube trays. Freeze until hard around
edges. Spoon mixture into large mixer
bowl or blender container; blend until
smooth. Pour into 1-quart mold;
freeze until firm, 4 to 6 hours. To serve,
unmold on chilled plate; cut into slices.
About 8 servings.

Bavarian Chocolate Pie

9-inch baked pastry shell or
   crumb crust
1 envelope unflavored gelatin
1⅔ cups milk, divided
⅔ cup sugar
⅓ cup HERSHEY'S Cocoa
2 tablespoons butter or
   margarine
¾ teaspoon vanilla extract
½ cup chilled whipping cream
   Spiced Cream (recipe follows)

Prepare pie shell; cool. In medium saucepan sprinkle gelatin over 1 cup milk; let stand 2 minutes to soften. Combine sugar and cocoa; add to mixture in saucepan. Cook over low heat, stirring constantly, until mixture boils. Remove from heat; add butter and stir until melted. Blend in remaining ⅔ cup milk and vanilla. Cool; chill until mixture begins to set, stirring occasionally. Beat cream until stiff; carefully fold into chocolate mixture. Pour into pie shell; chill until set. Garnish with Spiced Cream. *8 servings.*

Spiced Cream

In small mixer bowl combine ½ cup chilled whipping cream, 1 tablespoon confectioners' sugar, ¼ teaspoon vanilla extract, ¼ teaspoon ground cinnamon and dash ground nutmeg; beat until stiff. *About 1 cup topping.*

Chocolate Nut Crust ▶

1⅓ cups pie crust mix (½ of
   11-ounce package)
¼ cup packed light brown sugar
3 tablespoons HERSHEY'S Cocoa
¾ cup finely chopped walnuts
1 tablespoon water
1 tablespoon vegetable oil
1 teaspoon vanilla extract

Heat oven to 375.° In medium mixing bowl combine pie crust mix, sugar and cocoa. Stir in nuts. Combine water, oil and vanilla; drizzle over pie crust mixture while stirring with fork. (Mixture will be crumbly.) Press mixture evenly on bottom and up sides of 9-inch pie plate. Bake 15 minutes; cool.

Coffee Butter-Crunch Pie

Chocolate Nut Crust (recipe
  page 48)
2 teaspoons powdered instant
  coffee
1 teaspoon boiling water
½ cup unsalted butter, softened
¾ cup packed light brown sugar
3 tablespoons HERSHEY'S Cocoa
2 eggs
  Topping (recipe follows)
  Chocolate curls or grated
  chocolate (optional)

Prepare pie shell; cool. Dissolve
instant coffee in water; set aside. In
small mixer bowl cream butter. Add
sugar; beat on medium speed 3 minutes. Beat in cocoa and coffee mixture.
Add eggs, one at a time, beating 5 minutes after each addition, scraping sides
of bowl occasionally. Pour filling into
cooled crust. Cover and refrigerate 5
to 6 hours. Prepare Topping; spread
over top of filling. Refrigerate 1 hour
or until serving time. Garnish with
chocolate curls or grated chocolate,
if desired. Refrigerate leftovers.
8 servings.

Topping

In small mixer bowl combine ½ cup
chilled whipping cream, 1 tablespoon
confectioners' sugar and ¼ teaspoon
vanilla extract; beat until stiff.
About 1 cup topping.

VARIATIONS
Mile High Topping: In large mixer
bowl combine 2 cups chilled whipping
cream, ¼ cup confectioners' sugar
and 1 teaspoon vanilla extract; beat
just until cream holds a definite shape.
Do not over beat. Spread over top of
filling. Refrigerate at least 1 hour.

Mile High Coffee-Flavored Topping:
Increase confectioners' sugar to ½ cup.
Add 1 to 2 tablespoons powdered in-
stant coffee. Follow directions above.

Chocolate Cherry Surprise

14 ladyfingers, split*
1 envelope unflavored gelatin
½ cup cold milk
1 package (8 ounces) cream
    cheese, softened and at room
    temperature
⅔ cup sugar
1 teaspoon vanilla extract
¼ cup maraschino cherries,
    chopped
⅛ teaspoon almond extract
¼ cup HERSHEY'S Cocoa
1½ cups chilled whipping cream

Line loaf pan, 9x5x3 inches, with aluminum foil. Place ladyfingers on bottom and sides of foil-lined pan, cutting to fit where necessary; set aside. In small saucepan sprinkle gelatin over milk. Let stand 2 minutes to soften. Stir constantly over low heat until gelatin is completely dis-

solved, about 5 minutes. In large mixer bowl beat cream cheese, sugar and vanilla until smooth. Blend in gelatin mixture; mix well. Remove ⅓ cup mixture to small bowl; stir in cherries and almond extract. Add cocoa to remaining mixture in large bowl, blending well. Beat cream until stiff. Fold ½ cup whipped cream into cherry mixture; fold remaining whipped cream into chocolate. Spoon half of chocolate mixture into prepared pan. Using large serving spoon, make deep depression down the length of chocolate mixture in pan. Spoon cherry mixture into depression, mounding slightly. Spoon in remaining chocolate mixture. Cover; refrigerate until set, about 4 hours. To serve, unmold onto serving plate. Garnish as desired. *8 to 10 servings.*

*One 10¾-ounce frozen pound cake, thawed, and cut into ⅜ inch slices, may be substituted.

50

Jubilee Chocolate Cake

¾ teaspoon baking soda
1 cup buttermilk or sour milk*
1½ cups cake flour or 1¼ cups
    all-purpose flour
1½ cups sugar, divided
½ cup HERSHEY'S Cocoa
½ teaspoon salt
½ cup vegetable oil
2 eggs, separated
½ teaspoon vanilla extract
    Vanilla ice cream
    Flaming Cherry Sauce
    (recipe follows)

In medium bowl stir baking soda into buttermilk until dissolved; set aside. Heat oven to 350°. Grease and flour rectangular pan, 13x9x2 inches. In large mixer bowl combine flour, 1 cup sugar, cocoa and salt. Add oil, buttermilk mixture, egg yolks and vanilla; beat until smooth. In small mixer bowl beat egg whites until foamy; gradually add remaining ½ cup sugar, beating until stiff peaks form. Gently fold egg whites into chocolate batter. Pour into prepared pan. Bake 30 to 35 minutes or until cake springs back when touched lightly in center. Cool in pan. Cut into squares; top each square with scoop of ice cream and serving of Flaming Cherry Sauce. *Serves 10 to 12.*

*To sour milk: Use 1 tablespoon vinegar plus milk to equal 1 cup.

Flaming Cherry Sauce

1 can (16 or 17 ounces) pitted
    dark or light sweet cherries,
    drained (reserve ¾ cup liquid)
1½ tablespoons sugar
1 tablespoon cornstarch
    Dash salt
½ teaspoon grated orange peel
¼ cup kirsch or brandy

In saucepan or chafing dish combine reserved liquid with sugar, cornstarch and salt. Cook and stir until mixture thickens; boil 1 minute. Add cherries and orange peel; heat thoroughly.
In small saucepan over low heat gently heat kirsch or brandy; pour over cherry mixture. Ignite with match. Stir gently; serve as directed. *4 to 6 servings.* (Repeat procedure for sufficient amount of sauce for entire cake.)

Chocolate-Cherry Squares

1 cup all-purpose flour
⅓ cup butter or margarine
½ cup packed light brown sugar
½ cup chopped nuts
    Filling (recipe follows)
    Red candied cherries, halved

Heat oven to 350°. In large mixer bowl combine flour, butter and brown sugar. Blend on low speed to form fine crumbs, about 2 to 3 minutes. Stir in nuts. Reserve ¾ cup crumb mixture for topping; pat remaining crumbs into ungreased square pan, 9x9x2 inches. Bake 10 minutes or until lightly browned. Meanwhile, prepare Filling; spread over warm crust. Sprinkle with reserved crumb mixture; garnish with cherry halves. Return to oven: bake 25 minutes or until lightly browned. Cool; cut into squares. Store, covered, in refrigerator. *About 3 dozen squares.*

Filling

1 package (8 ounces) cream
    cheese, softened
½ cup sugar
⅓ cup HERSHEY'S Cocoa
¼ cup milk
1 egg
¼ teaspoon vanilla extract
¼ cup chopped red candied
    cherries

In small mixer bowl combine cream cheese and sugar; beat until fluffy. Add cocoa, milk, egg and vanilla; beat until smooth. Fold in cherries.

Chocolate Truffles

¾ cup butter
¾ cup HERSHEY'S Cocoa
1 can (14 ounces) sweetened
   condensed milk
1 tablespoon vanilla extract
   Cocoa or confectioners' sugar

In heavy saucepan over low heat melt butter. Add cocoa; stir until smooth. Blend in sweetened condensed milk; stir constantly until mixture is thick, smooth and glossy, about 4 minutes. Remove from heat; stir in vanilla. Chill 3 to 4 hours or until firm. Shape into 1¼-inch balls; roll in cocoa or confectioners' sugar. Chill until firm, 1 to 2 hours. Store, covered, in refrigerator. *About 2½ dozen candies.*

Nut Truffles: Add ¾ cup coarsely chopped toasted pecans to chocolate mixture when adding vanilla. (To toast pecans: In ungreased shallow pan spread ¾ cup pecan halves in single layer. Bake at 375° stirring occasionally, until golden brown, about 5 to 7 minutes.)

Rum Nut Truffles: Decrease vanilla to 1 teaspoon. Stir in 2 to 3 tablespoons rum or 1 teaspoon rum extract and nuts.

Espresso Truffles: Decrease vanilla to 1 teaspoon. Stir in 1¼ teaspoons instant espresso coffee with vanilla. Roll balls in cocoa or chopped nuts.

Nut-Coated Truffles: Roll balls in chopped nuts.

Black Forest Crepes

3 eggs
1 cup all-purpose flour
2 tablespoons HERSHEY'S Cocoa
2 tablespoons sugar
1¼ cups buttermilk
3 tablespoons melted butter
  Melted butter
  Cherry pie filling
  Sweetened whipped cream
  Chocolate Sauce (recipe
    follows)

In small mixer bowl beat eggs. Combine flour, cocoa and sugar; add to eggs alternately with buttermilk, beating until smooth. Beat in 3 tablespoons melted butter; chill about 1 hour. Heat small skillet or crepe pan (7-inch diameter) over medium heat; brush lightly with melted butter. For each crepe, pour about 2 tablespoons batter in pan; immediately rotate pan to evenly cover bottom. Cook until crepe surface begins to dry, about 1 minute; turn and cook other side. Stack crepes, placing wax paper between each. Refrigerate or freeze for later use, if desired. Just before serving, place 2 tablespoons pie filling in center of each crepe; fold edges over filling. Place in shallow oven-proof dish; heat in oven at 225° for 15 mintues.* Drizzle with Chocolate Sauce; top with dollop of sweetened whipped cream.
About 18 crepes.

*Microwave Heating Directions:
Place 8 filled crepes in shallow micro-proof dish. Microwave on high (full power) for 1 to 1½ minutes, or just until crepes are warm.

Chocolate Sauce

¾ cup sugar
⅓ cup HERSHEY'S Cocoa
¾ cup evaporated milk
¼ cup butter
⅛ teaspoon salt
1 teaspoon kirsch (optional)

In small saucepan combine sugar and cocoa; blend in evaporated milk, butter and salt. Cook over medium heat, stirring constantly, until mixture boils. Remove from heat; stir in kirsch. Serve warm. Cover and refrigerate leftover sauce. *About 1 cup sauce.*

Chocolate Butter Pecan Ice Cream

½ cup coarsely chopped pecans
1 tablespoon butter
½ cup HERSHEY'S Cocoa
⅔ cup water
1 can (14 ounces) sweetened
    condensed milk
2 teaspoons vanilla extract
2 cups chilled whipping cream

In small skillet over medium heat
sauté pecans in butter 2 minutes. Cool.
In small saucepan combine cocoa and
water; bring to boil over medium heat,
stirring constantly. Remove from heat;
stir in sweetened condensed milk and
vanilla. Pour into square pan, 9x9x2
inches; freeze until mushy. In large
mixer bowl beat cream until stiff.
In small chilled bowl whip chocolate
mixture; fold into whipped cream.
Blend in pecans. Return to square pan;
cover and return to freezer. Freeze, stirring frequently during first hour, until
firm. *About 1½ quarts ice cream.*

Chocolate Orange Balls

1 package (12 ounces) vanilla
    wafer cookies
¾ cup confectioners' sugar
1½ cups chopped nuts
¼ cup HERSHEY'S Cocoa
3 tablespoons light corn syrup
½ cup orange juice
1 teaspoon grated orange peel
    Confectioners' sugar

Finely crush vanilla wafer cookies.
In large mixing bowl combine crushed
wafers, ¾ cup confectioners' sugar,
nuts and cocoa. Blend in corn syrup,
orange juice and peel. Shape into 1-
inch balls; roll in confectioners' sugar.
Store in airtight container 2 to 3 days
to develop flavor. Roll again in confectioners' sugar before serving.
About 4 dozen balls.

Hershey's Cocoa Classics

Tried and true, old and new, these ever popular recipes are the most asked for favorites from the Hershey Kitchens since we first began creating delicious desserts over 30 years ago.

(Pictured: Black Magic Cake, recipe page 58.)

Black Magic Cake

1¾ cups all-purpose flour
2 cups sugar
¾ cup HERSHEY'S Cocoa
2 teaspoons baking soda
1 teaspoon baking powder
1 teaspoon salt
2 eggs
1 cup strong black coffee (or 2 teaspoons powdered instant coffee plus 1 cup boiling water)
1 cup buttermilk or sour milk*
½ cup vegetable oil
1 teaspoon vanilla extract

Heat oven to 350°. Grease and flour 2 round pans, 9x1½ inches or rectangular pan, 13x9x2 inches. In large mixer bowl combine flour, sugar, cocoa, baking soda, baking powder and salt. Add eggs, coffee, buttermilk, oil and vanilla; beat 2 minutes on medium speed (batter will be thin). Pour batter into prepared pan(s). Bake 30 to 35 minutes for round pans, 35 to 40 minutes for rectangular pan or until wooden pick inserted in center comes out clean. Cool 10 minutes; remove from pan(s). Cool completely; frost as desired. *10 to 12 servings.*

*To sour milk: Use 1 tablespoon vinegar plus milk to equal 1 cup.

Marble Cheesecake

Chocolate Crumb Crust
(recipe follows)
3 packages (8 ounces each) cream cheese, softened
1 cup sugar, divided
½ cup dairy sour cream
2½ teaspoons vanilla extract, divided
3 tablespoons all-purpose flour
3 eggs
¼ cup HERSHEY'S Cocoa
1 tablespoon vegetable oil

Prepare Chocolate Crumb Crust; set aside. Heat oven to 450°. In large mixer bowl combine cream cheese, ¾ cup sugar, sour cream and 2 teaspoons vanilla; beat on medium speed until smooth. Gradually add flour; blend well. Add eggs and beat well; set aside. In small bowl combine cocoa and remaining ¼ cup sugar. Add oil, remaining ½ teaspoon vanilla and 1½ cups of cream cheese mixture; blend well. Spoon plain and chocolate mixtures alternately into cooled crust, ending with dollops of chocolate on top; gently swirl with knife or spatula for marbled effect. Bake 10 minutes. Without opening oven door, decrease temperature to 250° and continue to bake 30 minutes. Turn off oven; leave cheesecake in oven 30 minutes without opening door. Remove from oven; loosen cake from side of pan. Cool completely; cover and refrigerate. *10 to 12 servings.*

Chocolate Crumb Crust

1 cup vanilla wafer crumbs
¼ cup confectioners' sugar
¼ cup **HERSHEY'S Cocoa**
¼ cup **butter or margarine, melted**

Heat oven to 350°. In medium bowl combine crumbs, confectioners' sugar and cocoa. Stir in melted butter. Press mixture on bottom and ½ inch up side of 9-inch springform pan. Bake 8 minutes; cool.

To Marble: Spoon plain and chocolate mixtures alternately into cooled crust, ending with dollops of chocolate on top; gently swirl with knife or spatula for marbled effect.

Meringue-Topped Chocolate Cream Pie

9-inch baked pastry shell
1 cup sugar
½ cup all-purpose flour
6 tablespoons HERSHEY'S Cocoa
½ teaspoon salt
2 cups milk
3 egg yolks, slightly beaten
¼ cup butter or margarine
2 teaspoons vanilla extract
Meringue Topping (recipe follows)

Prepare pie shell; cool. In medium saucepan combine sugar, flour, cocoa and salt; stir in milk. Cook over medium heat, stirring constantly, until mixture boils; remove from heat. Stir half of mixture into beaten egg yolks; return mixture to saucepan. Continue cooking and stirring over medium heat until mixture boils; boil and stir 1 minute. Remove from heat; stir in butter and vanilla. Press plastic wrap directly onto surface. Cool 10 minutes; pour into pie shell. Heat oven to 350.° Meanwhile, prepare Meringue Topping; spread on warm filling, carefully sealing to edges of crust. Bake 5 to 8 minutes or just until meringue is lightly browned. Cool to room temperature; chill several hours. Refrigerate leftovers. *8 servings.*

Meringue Topping: In small mixer bowl beat 4 egg whites and ½ teaspoon cream of tartar until foamy. Gradually add 6 tablespoons sugar; beat until stiff peaks form.

Chocolatetown Special Cake

½ cup HERSHEY'S Cocoa
½ cup boiling water
⅔ cup shortening
1¾ cups sugar
1 teaspoon vanilla extract
2 eggs
2¼ cups all-purpose flour
1½ teaspoons baking soda
½ teaspoon salt
1⅓ cups buttermilk or sour milk*
One-Bowl Buttercream Frosting
(recipe follows)

In small bowl stir together cocoa and boiling water until smooth; set aside. Heat oven to 350° Grease and flour 2 round pans, 9 x 1½ inches. In large mixer bowl cream shortening, sugar and vanilla until light and fluffy. Add eggs; beat well. Combine flour, baking soda and salt; add alternately with buttermilk to creamed mixture. Blend in cocoa mixture. Pour into prepared pans. Bake 35 to 40 minutes or until wooden pick inserted in center comes out clean. Cool 10 minutes; remove from pans. Cool completely; frost with One-Bowl Buttercream Frosting. *10 to 12 servings.*

*To sour milk: Use 1 tablespoon plus 1 teaspoon vinegar plus milk to equal 1⅓ cups.

One-Bowl Buttercream Frosting:
In small mixer bowl cream 6 tablespoons butter or margarine, softened. Add 2⅔ cups confectioners' sugar and ½ cup HERSHEY'S Cocoa alternately with ⅓ cup milk; beat to spreading consistency (additional milk may be needed). Blend in 1 teaspoon vanilla extract. *About 2 cups frosting.*

61

1. *Place on lightly greased cookie sheet. Press thumb gently in center of each cookie.*

2. *As soon as cookies are removed from oven, spoon about ¼ teaspoon filling in thumbprint.*

3. *Gently press unwrapped KISS in center of each cookie.*

Chocolate Thumbprint Cookies

½ cup butter or margarine
⅔ cup sugar
1 egg, separated
2 tablespoons milk
1 teaspoon vanilla extract
1 cup all-purpose flour
⅓ cup HERSHEY'S Cocoa
¼ teaspoon salt
1 cup chopped nuts
   Vanilla Filling (recipe follows)
26 HERSHEY'S KISSES,
   unwrapped, or pecan halves
   or candied cherry halves

In small mixer bowl cream butter, sugar, egg yolk, milk and vanilla. Combine flour, cocoa and salt; blend into creamed mixture. Chill dough at least 1 hour or until firm enough to handle. Heat oven to 350.° Shape dough into 1-inch balls. Beat egg white slightly. Dip each ball into egg white; roll in nuts. Place on lightly greased cookie sheet. Press thumb gently in center of each cookie. Bake 10 to 12 minutes or until set. As soon as cookies are removed from oven, spoon about ¼ teaspoon filling in thumbprint. Gently press unwrapped KISS or pecan or cherry in center of each cookie. Carefully remove from cookie sheet; cool on wire rack. *About 2 dozen cookies.*

Vanilla Filling: In small mixing bowl combine ½ cup confectioners' sugar, 1 tablespoon butter or margarine, softened, 2 teaspoons milk and ¼ teaspoon vanilla extract; beat until smooth.

Cocoa KISS Cookies

1 cup butter or margarine,
    softened
$2/3$ cup sugar
1 teaspoon vanilla extract
$1\,2/3$ cups all-purpose flour
$1/4$ cup HERSHEY'S Cocoa
1 cup finely chopped pecans
54 HERSHEY'S KISSES (9-ounce
    package), unwrapped
Confectioners' sugar

In large mixer bowl cream butter,
sugar and vanilla until light and fluffy.
Combine flour and cocoa; blend into
creamed mixture. Add nuts; beat
on low speed until well blended.
Chill dough 1 hour or until firm
enough to handle. Heat oven to
375°. Mold scant tablespoon
of dough around each un-
wrapped KISS, covering KISS
completely. Shape into balls;
place on ungreased cookie
sheet. Bake 10 to 12 minutes or
until almost set. Cool slightly;
remove from cookie sheet onto
wire rack. Cool completely. Roll in
confectioners' sugar. *About 4½
dozen cookies.*

Aztec Sunburst Cake

¾ cup plus 2 tablespoons butter
  or margarine, divided
½ cup packed light brown sugar
2 tablespoons light corn syrup
1 can (16 ounces) pear halves,
  4 to 6 halves
7 maraschino cherries, cut into
  quarters
¼ cup chopped pecans
1¼ cups sugar
1 teaspoon vanilla extract
2 eggs
1½ cups all-purpose flour
¼ cup HERSHEY'S Cocoa
½ teaspoon baking soda
½ teaspoon salt
½ cup buttermilk or sour milk*
  Sweetened whipped cream
  (optional)

Heat oven to 350° In square pan, 9x9x2 inches, melt ¼ cup butter in oven. Stir in brown sugar and corn syrup; spread evenly in pan. Drain pear halves; slice each half lengthwise into 4 sections, if desired, and place in sunburst design over mixture in pan. Arrange cherries and pecans between pear sections, in center and at corners. In large mixer bowl cream remaining ½ cup plus 2 tablespoons butter, sugar and vanilla. Add eggs; beat well. Combine flour, cocoa, baking soda and salt; add alternately with buttermilk to creamed mixture. Carefully pour batter over fruit and nuts in pan. Bake 50 to 55 minutes or until wooden pick inserted in center comes out clean. Immediately invert onto serving plate. Serve warm or cold with sweetened whipped cream, if desired.
8 to 10 servings.

*To sour milk: Use 1½ teaspoons vinegar plus milk to equal ½ cup.

Collector's Cocoa Cake

¾ cup butter or margarine
1¾ cups sugar
2 eggs
1 teaspoon vanilla extract
2 cups all-purpose flour
¾ cup HERSHEY'S Cocoa
1¼ teaspoons baking soda
½ teaspoon salt
1⅓ cups water
Peanut Butter Cream Frosting
(recipe follows)

Heat oven to 350°. Grease and flour 2 round pans, 8 or 9 x 1½ inches. In large mixer bowl cream butter and sugar. Add eggs and vanilla; beat 1 minute at medium speed. Combine flour, cocoa, baking soda and salt; add alternately with water to creamed mixture, beating after each addition. Pour batter into prepared pans. Bake 35 to 40 minutes for 8-inch rounds, 30 to 35 minutes for 9-inch rounds or until wooden pick inserted in center comes out clean. Cool 10 minutes; remove from pans. Cool completely; frost with Peanut Butter Cream Frosting. Cover and refrigerate frosted cake. *8 to 10 servings.*

Peanut Butter Cream Frosting

In top of double boiler over hot, not boiling, water combine 2 cups (12-ounce package) REESE'S Peanut Butter Chips, ⅔ cup milk and 3 cups miniature marshmallows. Stir until marshmallows and chips are melted and mixture is smooth. Cool to lukewarm. In large mixer bowl beat 2 cups chilled whipping cream and ½ teaspoon vanilla extract until stiff; fold in cooled peanut butter mixture. *About 5 cups frosting.*

Best Brownies

½ cup butter or margarine, melted
1 cup sugar
1 teaspoon vanilla extract
2 eggs
½ cup all-purpose flour
⅓ cup HERSHEY'S Cocoa
¼ teaspoon baking powder
¼ teaspoon salt
½ cup chopped nuts (optional)
   Creamy Brownie Frosting
   (optional, recipe follows)

Heat oven to 350° Grease square pan, 9x9x2 inches. In large mixing bowl blend melted butter, sugar and vanilla. Add eggs; using spoon, beat well. Combine flour, cocoa, baking powder and salt; gradually blend into egg mixture. Stir in nuts, if desired. Spread into prepared pan. Bake 20 to 25 minutes or until brownies begin to pull away from sides of pan. Cool; frost with Creamy Brownie Frosting, if desired. Cut into squares. *About 16 brownies.*

Creamy Brownie Frosting

3 tablespoons butter or
   margarine, softened
3 tablespoons HERSHEY'S Cocoa
1 tablespoon light corn syrup
   or honey
½ teaspoon vanilla extract
1 cup confectioners' sugar
1 to 2 tablespoons milk

In small mixing bowl cream butter, cocoa, corn syrup and vanilla. Add confectioners' sugar and milk; beat to spreading consistency.
About 1 cup frosting.

Rich Cocoa Fudge

3 cups sugar
⅔ cup HERSHEY'S Cocoa
⅛ teaspoon salt
1½ cups milk
¼ cup butter or margarine
1 teaspoon vanilla extract

Butter square pan, 8x8x2 or 9x9x2 inches; set aside. In heavy 4-quart saucepan combine sugar, cocoa and salt; stir in milk. Cook over medium heat, stirring constantly, until mixture comes to full rolling boil. Boil, without stirring, to 234°F (soft-ball stage) or until syrup, when dropped into very cold water, forms soft ball which flattens when removed from water. (Bulb of candy thermometer should not rest on bottom of saucepan.) Remove from heat. Add butter and vanilla. DO NOT STIR. Cool at room temperature to 110°F (lukewarm). Beat until fudge thickens and loses some of its gloss. Quickly spread into prepared pan; cool. Cut into squares.
About 3 dozen candies.

VARIATIONS:
Nutty Rich Cocoa Fudge: Beat cooked fudge as directed. Immediately stir in 1 cup broken almonds, pecans or walnuts and quickly spread into prepared pan.

Marshmallow-Nut Fudge: Increase cocoa to ¾ cup; cook fudge as directed above. Add 1 cup marshmallow creme with butter and vanilla. DO NOT STIR. Cool to 110°F (lukewarm). Beat 10 minutes; stir in 1 cup broken nuts and pour into prepared pan. (Fudge does not set until poured into pan.)

Quick And Easy Chocolate

Many of these quick and easy recipes can be mixed in one bowl and are ready for the oven in just five minutes.

(Pictured: Chocolate Mousse Parfaits, Chocolate Mint Mousse in Chocolate Party Cups, Chocolate Mousse Filled Croissants, recipes page 70.)

1 teaspoon unflavored gelatin
1 tablespoon cold water
2 tablespoons boiling water
½ cup sugar
¼ cup **HERSHEY'S** Cocoa
1 cup chilled whipping cream
1 teaspoon vanilla extract

In small bowl sprinkle gelatin over cold water; let stand 1 minute to soften. Add boiling water; stir until gelatin is completely dissolved and mixture is clear. Cool slightly. In small cold mixer bowl stir together sugar and cocoa; add whipping cream and vanilla. Beat at medium speed, scraping bottom of bowl occasionally, until stiff peaks form; pour in gelatin mixture and beat until well blended. Spoon into serving dishes. Chill about ½ hour.
Four ½ cup servings.

Double Recipe: Use 1 envelope gelatin; double remaining ingredients. Follow directions above; use large cold mixer bowl.

Chocolate Mousse Parfaits: Prepare Chocolate Mousse according to directions. Alternately spoon mousse and sliced or diced fresh fruit into parfait glasses. (Strawberries, peaches or nectarines are good. About 1½ cups prepared fruit will be needed.) Chill about 1 hour. *5 to 6 servings.*

Variation: Substitute chilled cherry pie filling for fresh fruit.

Chocolate Mint Mousse in Chocolate Party Cups: Prepare one-half recipe Chocolate Party Cups (recipe page 119). Prepare Chocolate Mousse according to directions reducing vanilla extract to ½ teaspoon; add ⅛ to ¼ teaspoon mint extract. Spoon or pipe into chocolate cups; chill 2 to 3 hours. *6 servings.*

Chocolate Mousse Filled Croissants: Prepare Chocolate Mousse according to directions. Cut 6 bakery croissants horizontally in half. Spread about ⅓ cup mousse on each bottom half; replace top halves of croissants. Chill about ½ hour. To serve, top filled croissants with desired flavor canned fruit pie filling. *6 servings.*

High-Rise Chocolate Mousse: Measure length of aluminum foil to fit around individual 3- or 4-ounce dessert dishes, custard cups or parfait glasses. Cut and fold foil to double thickness for collar. Lightly oil one side of foil; tape securely to outside of dish (oiled side in) allowing collar to extend 2 inches above rim. Prepare Double Recipe. Spoon mixture into prepared dishes. Chill 2 to 3 hours. Just before serving, carefully remove foil. Gently press chopped nuts onto side of mousse. *4 to 6 servings.*

Chocolate Mousse Pie with Rum Cream Topping: Prepare and bake 8- or 9-inch pastry shell or crumb crust. Prepare Chocolate Mousse according to directions. Pour into cooled shell or crust. In small mixer bowl beat 1 cup chilled whipping cream, 2 tablespoons confectioners' sugar and 2 teaspoons light rum or ¼ teaspoon rum extract until stiff. Spread topping over mousse. Chill at least 2 hours. Garnish as desired. *6 to 8 servings.*

Pound Cake Torte: Prepare Chocolate Mousse according to directions. Slice loaf pound cake horizontally into 3 layers. Spread mousse evenly over one side of each cake layer. Stack layers. Chill 1 to 2 hours. Garnish with sliced nuts or fruit. *8 to 10 servings.*

▼Deep Dark Chocolate Cake

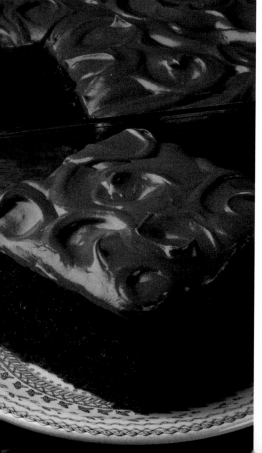

2 cups sugar
1¾ cups all-purpose flour
¾ cup HERSHEY'S Cocoa
1½ teaspoons baking soda
1½ teaspoons baking powder
1 teaspoon salt
2 eggs
1 cup milk
½ cup vegetable oil
2 teaspoons vanilla extract
1 cup boiling water
One-Bowl Buttercream
Frosting (recipe follows)

Heat oven 350° Grease and flour 2 round pans, 9x1½ inches or rectangular pan, 13x9x2 inches. In large mixer bowl combine dry ingredients. Add eggs, milk, oil and vanilla; beat on medium speed 2 minutes. Remove from mixer; stir in boiling water (batter will be thin). Pour into prepared pan(s). Bake 30 to 35 minutes for round pans, 35 to 40 minutes for rectangular pan or until wooden pick inserted in center comes out clean. Cool cake in rounds 10 minutes; remove from pans. Cool completely. (Do not remove cake from rectangular pan.) Frost with One-Bowl Buttercream Frosting. *8 to 10 servings.*

One-Bowl Buttercream Frosting

6 tablespoons butter or
margarine, softened
HERSHEY'S Cocoa:
⅓ cup for light flavor
½ cup for medium flavor
¾ cup for dark flavor
2⅔ cups confectioners' sugar
⅓ cup milk
1 teaspoon vanilla extract

In small mixer bowl cream butter. Add cocoa and confectioners' sugar alternately with milk; beat to spreading consistency (additional milk may be needed). Blend in vanilla. *About 2 cups frosting.*

VARIATIONS:

Chocolate Cupcakes

Prepare Deep Dark Chocolate Cake as directed. Fill paper-lined muffin cups (2½ inches in diameter) ⅔ full with batter. Bake at 350° for 18 to 22 minutes or until wooden pick inserted in center comes out clean. Cool; frost as desired. *About 3 dozen cupcakes.*

Black Forest Torte (Top), Triple Layer Mousse Cake (Bottom), Recipes page 74.

73

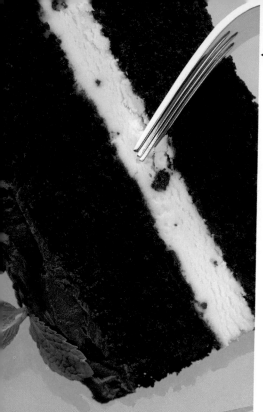

◄ Ice Cream Cake

3 cups ice cream, softened
  Deep Dark Chocolate Cake
    (recipe page 72)
  One-Bowl Buttercream Frosting
    (recipe page 72) OR 1 container
    (8 ounces) frozen whipped
    topping, thawed

Line 1 round pan, 9 x 1½ inches, with aluminum foil. Firmly pack ice cream into pan. Cover; freeze about 3 hours. Bake cake in 2 round pans, 9 x 1½ inches as directed. Cool 10 minutes; remove from pans. Cool completely. Place one cake layer upside down on serving plate. Top with ice cream layer unmolded from cake pan; peel off foil. Place second cake layer, top side up, over ice cream layer. Gently spread One-Bowl Buttercream Frosting or whipped topping on top and side of cake. Cover and freeze at least 1 hour before serving. *10 to 12 servings.*

Triple Layer Chocolate Mousse Cake

Deep Dark Chocolate Cake (recipe
    page 72)
Chocolate Mousse, Double Recipe
    (recipe page 70)
Sliced almonds (optional)
Chocolate curls (optional)

Bake cake in 3 round pans, 8 x 1½ inches, at 350° for 30 to 35 minutes. Cool 10 minutes; remove from pans. Cool completely. Prepare Chocolate Mousse, Double Recipe, according to directions. Fill and frost layers with mousse. Garnish with sliced almonds and chocolate curls, if desired. Refrigerate at least 1 hour. Cover and refrigerate remaining cake. *10 to 12 servings.*

Black Forest Torte

Deep Dark Chocolate Cake
    (recipe page 72)
1 can (21 ounces) cherry pie filling,
    chilled
1 container (4 ounces) frozen
    whipped topping, thawed

Bake cake in 2 round pans, 9 x 1½ inches, as directed. Cool 10 minutes; remove from pans. Cool completely. Place one layer on serving plate. Spoon half of pie filling in center and spread to within ½ inch of edge. Spoon or pipe border of whipped topping around edge. Top with second layer. Spoon remaining pie filling to within ½ inch of edge. Make border around top edge with remaining topping. Chill. *10 to 12 servings.*

Cocoa Bundt Cake

1⅔ cups all-purpose flour
1½ cups sugar
  ½ cup HERSHEY'S Cocoa
1½ teaspoons baking soda
  ½ teaspoon baking powder
  1 teaspoon salt
  2 eggs
  ½ cup shortening
1½ cups buttermilk or sour milk*
  1 teaspoon vanilla extract
    Cocoa Glaze (recipe follows)

Heat oven to 350°. Generously grease and flour 12-cup Bundt pan.** In large mixer bowl blend flour, sugar, cocoa, baking soda, baking powder and salt; add remaining ingredients except Cocoa Glaze. Beat on low speed 1 minute, scraping bowl constantly. Beat on high speed 3 minutes, scraping bowl occasionally. Pour into prepared pan. Bake 50 to 55 minutes or until wooden pick inserted in center comes out clean. Cool 10 minutes; remove from pan to wire rack. Cool completely. Drizzle with Cocoa Glaze. *12 to 16 servings.*

*To sour milk: Use 1½ tablespoons vinegar plus milk to equal 1½ cups.

**Or pour batter into greased and floured rectangular pan, 13x9x2 inches. Bake at 350° for 35 to 40 minutes or until wooden pick inserted in center comes out clean. Cool completely; frost with One-Bowl Buttercream Frosting (recipe page 72).

Cocoa Glaze

2 tablespoons butter or margarine
2 tablespoons HERSHEY'S Cocoa
2 tablespoons water
1 cup confectioners' sugar
½ teaspoon vanilla extract

In small saucepan over low heat melt butter; add cocoa and water, stirring constantly, until mixture thickens. Do not boil. Remove from heat; gradually add confectioners' sugar and vanilla, beating with wire whisk until smooth. Add additional water, ½ teaspoon at a time, until desired consistency. *About ¾ cup glaze.*

Fast Chocolate-Pecan ◄ Fudge

½ cup butter or margarine
¾ cup HERSHEY'S Cocoa
4 cups confectioners' sugar
1 teaspoon vanilla extract
½ cup evaporated milk
1 cup pecan pieces

Line square pan, 8x8x2 inches, with aluminum foil; set aside. In 2-quart micro-proof bowl microwave butter on high (full power) 1 to 1½ minutes or until melted. Add cocoa; stir until smooth. Stir in confectioners' sugar and vanilla; blend well (mixture will be dry and crumbly). Stir in evaporated milk. Microwave on high 1 to 2 minutes or until mixture is hot. Stir until smooth; add pecan pieces. Pour into prepared pan. Cover; chill until firm. Cut into squares. Store, covered, in refrigerator. *4 dozen squares.*

Conventional Directions: Prepare pan as above. In medium saucepan melt butter. Remove from heat; stir in cocoa. Stir in confectioners' sugar and vanilla; add evaporated milk. Stir constantly over low heat until warm and smooth; add pecan pieces. Pour into prepared pan; chill and store as above.

Chocolate Cream Pie

1 package (3 ounces) cream cheese, softened
½ cup sugar
1 teaspoon vanilla extract
⅓ cup HERSHEY'S Cocoa
⅓ cup milk
1 container (8 ounces) frozen non-dairy whipped topping, thawed
8-inch (6 ounces) packaged graham crumb crust

In small mixer bowl combine cream cheese, sugar and vanilla until blended. Add cocoa alternately with milk, beating until smooth. Gradually fold in whipped topping until well combined. Spoon into pie shell. Cover; refrigerate until set, 4 to 6 hours. *6 to 8 servings.*

Deep Dish Brownies

¾ cup butter or margarine, melted
1½ cups sugar
1½ teaspoons vanilla extract
3 eggs
¾ cup all-purpose flour
½ cup HERSHEY'S Cocoa
½ teaspoon baking powder
½ teaspoon salt

Heat oven to 350° Grease square pan, 8x8x2 inches. In medium mixing bowl blend melted butter, sugar and vanilla. Add eggs; beat well with spoon. Combine flour, cocoa, baking powder and salt; gradually add to egg mixture, beating until well blended. Spread into prepared pan. Bake 40 to 45 minutes or until brownies begin to pull away from sides of pan. Cool completely; cut into squares. *16 brownies.*

Variation: Add 1 cup REESE'S Peanut Butter Chips or HERSHEY'S Semi-Sweet Chocolate Chips to batter.

Chocolate Rewards

*I*ndulge your taste for America's favorite flavor with these extra rich chocolatey delights.

(Pictured: Crème de Cacao Pie, recipe page 88.)

Fudge Brownie Pie

2 eggs
1 cup sugar
½ cup butter or margarine, melted
½ cup all-purpose flour
⅓ cup HERSHEY'S Cocoa
¼ teaspoon salt
1 teaspoon vanilla extract
½ cup chopped nuts (optional)
  Ice Cream
  Hot Fudge Sauce (recipe follows)

Heat oven to 350°. In small mixer bowl beat eggs; blend in sugar and melted butter. Combine flour, cocoa and salt; add to butter mixture. Stir in vanilla and nuts, if desired. Pour into lightly greased 8-inch pie plate. Bake 25 to 30 minutes or until almost set. (Pie will not test done in center.) Cool; cut into wedges. Serve topped with scoop of ice cream and drizzled with Hot Fudge Sauce. *6 to 8 servings.*

Hot Fudge Sauce

¾ cup sugar
½ cup HERSHEY'S Cocoa
½ cup plus 2 tablespoons (5-ounce
  can) evaporated milk
⅓ cup light corn syrup
⅓ cup butter or margarine
1 teaspoon vanilla extract

In small saucepan combine sugar and cocoa; blend in evaporated milk and corn syrup. Cook over medium heat, stirring constantly, until mixture boils; boil and stir 1 minute. Remove from heat; stir in butter and vanilla. Serve warm. *About 1¾ cups sauce.*

Microwave Directions: In medium micro-proof bowl combine all sauce ingredients except butter and vanilla. Microwave on high (full power) 1 to 3 minutes, stirring often, until mixture boils. Stir in butter and vanilla. Cool slightly; serve warm.

Cocoa Cheesecake

Graham Crust (recipe follows)
2 packages (8 ounces each) cream
   cheese, softened
¾ cup plus 2 tablespoons sugar,
   divided
½ cup HERSHEY'S Cocoa
2 teaspoons vanilla extract,
   divided
2 eggs
1 cup dairy sour cream

Prepare Graham Crust; set aside. Heat oven to 375.° In large mixer bowl beat cream cheese, ¾ cup sugar, cocoa and 1 teaspoon vanilla until light and fluffy. Add eggs; blend well. Pour into prepared crust. Bake 20 minutes. Remove from oven; cool 15 minutes. Increase oven temperature to 425.° Combine sour cream, remaining 2 tablespoons sugar and remaining 1 teaspoon vanilla; stir until smooth. Spread evenly over baked filling. Bake 10 minutes. Cool; refrigerate several hours or overnight. *10 to 12 servings.*

Graham Crust

Combine 1 ½ cups graham cracker crumbs, ⅓ cup sugar and ⅓ cup melted butter or margarine. Press mixture onto bottom and halfway up side of 9-inch springfoam pan.

Chocolate Lover's Cheesecake:
Prepare as above, adding 1 cup HERSHEY'S Semi-Sweet Chocolate Chips after eggs have been blended into mixture. Bake and serve as directed.

Chocolate Petits Fours

4 eggs, separated
¾ cup sugar, divided
¾ cup ground blanched almonds
⅓ cup all-purpose flour
⅓ cup HERSHEY'S Cocoa
½ teaspoon baking soda
¼ teaspoon salt
¼ cup water
1 teaspoon vanilla extract
¼ teaspoon almond extract
  Milk Chocolate or Semi-Sweet
    Chocolate Glaze (recipes
    page 86)
  Assorted decorating icing or gel

Heat oven to 375.° Line 15½ x 10½ x 1-inch jelly roll pan with aluminum foil; generously grease foil. In small mixer bowl beat egg yolks on medium speed 3 minutes. Gradually add ½ cup sugar; continue beating 2 minutes. Combine almonds, flour, cocoa, baking soda and salt; add alternately with water to egg yolk mixture, beating just until blended. Stir in vanilla and almond extract. In large mixer bowl beat egg whites until foamy; gradually add remaining ¼ cup sugar and continue beating until stiff peaks form. Carefully fold chocolate mixture into egg whites. Spread batter evenly in prepared pan. Bake 16 to 18 minutes or until top springs back when touched lightly. Carefully invert onto towel on cooling rack; remove foil. Cool.

To prepare Petits Fours: With small cookie cutters (approximately 1½-inch shapes) cut cake into assorted shapes. Place on wire rack with wax paper-covered cookie sheet below to catch drips when glazing. Prepare either Milk Chocolate or Semi-Sweet Chocolate Glaze. Spoon glaze over cake pieces until entire piece is covered. (Glaze that drips off can be reheated and used again.) Chill until glaze is set. Pipe decorations with icing or gel. Cover; store in cool place.
About 2 dozen petits fours.

Ultimate Chocolate Brownies

¾ cup HERSHEY'S Cocoa
½ teaspoon baking soda
⅔ cup butter or margarine, melted
    and divided
½ cup boiling water
2 cups sugar
2 eggs
1⅓ cups all-purpose flour
1 teaspoon vanilla extract
¼ teaspoon salt
1 cup HERSHEY'S Semi-Sweet
    Chocolate Chips
One-Bowl Buttercream Frosting
(recipe page 72)

Heat oven to 350°. Grease rectangular pan, 13x9x2 inches, or two square pans, 8x8x2 inches. In medium bowl combine cocoa and baking soda. Blend in ⅓ cup melted butter. Add boiling water; stir until mixture thickens. Stir in sugar, eggs and remaining ⅓ cup melted butter; stir until smooth. Add flour, vanilla and salt; blend completely. Stir in chocolate chips. Pour into prepared pan(s). Bake 35 to 40 minutes for rectangular pan, 30 to 35 minutes for square pans or until brownies begin to pull away from sides of pan. Cool completely in pan(s); frost with One-Bowl Buttercream Frosting. Cut into squares.
About 3 dozen brownies.

All-Chocolate Boston Cream Pie

1 cup all-purpose flour
1 cup sugar
1/3 cup HERSHEY'S Cocoa
1/2 teaspoon baking soda
6 tablespoons butter or
    margarine, softened
1 cup milk
1 egg
1 teaspoon vanilla extract
    Chocolate Filling (recipe follows)
    Satiny Chocolate Glaze (recipe
    follows)

Heat oven to 350°. Grease and flour round pan, 9 x 1 1/2 inches. In large mixer bowl combine flour, sugar, cocoa and baking soda. Add butter, milk, egg and vanilla. Blend on low speed until all ingredients are moistened. Beat on medium speed 2 minutes or until mixture is smooth. Pour into prepared pan. Bake 30 to 35 minutes or until wooden pick inserted in center comes out clean. Cool 10 minutes; remove from pan. Cool completely. Meanwhile, prepare Chocolate Filling. Cut cake horizontally into two thin layers. Spread filling over one cake layer; top with remaining layer. Cover; refrigerate. Pour Chocolate Glaze on top of cake, allowing some to drizzle down side. Cover; refrigerate. *8 servings.*

Satiny Chocolate Glaze

In small saucepan over low heat melt 2 tablespoons butter or margarine. Add 3 tablespoons HERSHEY'S Cocoa and 2 tablespoons water; stir constantly until mixture thickens. Do not boil. Remove from heat; add 1/2 teaspoon vanilla extract. Gradually add 1 cup confectioners' sugar, beating with wire whisk until smooth. *About 3/4 cup glaze.*

Chocolate Filling

1/2 cup sugar
1/4 cup HERSHEY'S Cocoa
2 tablespoons cornstarch
1 1/2 cups light cream or
    half-and-half
1 tablespoon butter or margarine
1 teaspoon vanilla extract

In medium saucepan combine sugar, cocoa and cornstarch; gradually add light cream. Cook and stir over medium heat until mixture thickens and begins to boil; boil and stir 1 minute. Remove from heat; blend in butter and vanilla. Press plastic wrap directly onto surface. Cool; refrigerate.

Chocolate Pots de Crème

2/3 cup sugar
6 tablespoons HERSHEY'S Cocoa
1 cup light cream
2 egg yolks, slightly beaten
1/4 cup butter, softened
1 teaspoon vanilla extract
    Sweetened whipped cream

In medium saucepan combine sugar and cocoa; gradually add light cream. Cook over medium heat, stirring constantly, just until mixture comes to a boil. Remove from heat; gradually stir into beaten egg yolks. Stir in butter and vanilla; blend well. Pour into six crème pots or demitasse cups; press plastic wrap directly onto surface. Chill several hours or until set. Garnish with sweetened whipped cream. *6 servings.*

All-Chocolate Boston Cream Pie (Top); Chocolate Pots de Crème (Bottom).

85

Milk Chocolate Glaze

One 8-ounce HERSHEY'S Milk
   Chocolate Bar
2 tablespoons vegetable
   shortening

Break bar into pieces. In top of double
boiler over hot, not boiling, water melt
chocolate pieces and shortening, stirring until smooth. Cool slightly, stirring
occasionally.

Semi-Sweet
Chocolate Glaze:

1 cup HERSHEY'S Semi-Sweet
   Chocolate Chips
¼ cup unsalted butter
2 teaspoons vegetable oil

In top of double boiler over hot, not
boiling, water melt chocolate chips with
butter and oil, stirring until smooth.
Cool slightly, stirring occasionally.

◄Chocolate-Amaretto Ice

¾ cup sugar
½ cup HERSHEY'S Cocoa
2 cups light cream or half-and-half
2 tablespoons almond flavored
   liqueur
Sliced almonds

In small saucepan combine sugar and
cocoa; gradually stir in light cream.
Cook over low heat, stirring constantly,
until sugar dissolves and mixture is
smooth and hot; do not boil. Remove
from heat; stir in liqueur. Pour into
square pan, 8x8x2 inches. Cover;
freeze until firm, stirring several times
before mixture freezes. Scoop into
dessert dishes. Serve frozen. Garnish
with sliced almonds. *4 servings.*

Fudgey Pecan Torte

  1 cup butter or margarine, melted
1½ cups sugar
1½ teaspoons vanilla extract
  3 eggs, separated and at room
      temperature
  ⅔ cup HERSHEY'S Cocoa
  ½ cup all-purpose flour
  3 tablespoons water
  ¾ cup finely chopped pecans
  ⅛ teaspoon cream of tartar
  ⅛ teaspoon salt
    Royal Glaze (recipe follows)
    Pecan halves (optional)

Line bottom of 9-inch springform pan with aluminum foil; butter foil and side of pan. Heat oven to 350°. In large mixer bowl combine melted butter, sugar and vanilla; beat well. Add egg yolks, one at a time, beating well after each addition. Blend in cocoa, flour and water; beat well. Stir in nuts. In small mixer bowl beat egg whites, cream of tartar and salt until stiff peaks form; carefully fold into chocolate mixture. Pour into prepared pan. Bake 45 minutes or until top begins to crack slightly. (Cake will not test done in center.) Cool 1 hour. Cover, chill until firm. Remove side of pan. Pour Royal Glaze over cake, allowing glaze to run down side. Spread glaze evenly on top and side. Allow to set. Garnish with pecan halves, if desired. *10 to 12 servings.*

ROYAL GLAZE

In small saucepan combine 1⅓ cups HERSHEY'S Semi-Sweet Chocolate Chips and ½ cup whipping cream. Cook over very low heat, stirring constantly, until chips are melted and mixture begins to thicken.

Crème de Cacao Pie

9-inch baked pastry shell
1 envelope unflavored gelatin
½ cup cold milk
¼ cup butter or margarine
⅔ cup sugar, divided
6 tablespoons HERSHEY'S Cocoa
3 eggs, separated and at room
    temperature
¼ cup crème de cacao

Prepare pie shell; cool. In small bowl sprinkle gelatin over milk; let stand 5 minutes to soften. In medium saucepan over low heat melt butter; remove from heat. Stir in ⅓ cup sugar and cocoa. Add gelatin mixture; blend well. Slightly beat egg yolks; stir into chocolate mixture. Cook over medium heat, stirring constantly, until mixture is hot and gelatin is dissolved. Do not boil. Remove from heat; stir in crème de cacao. Cool to room temperature, stirring occasionally. In large mixer bowl beat egg whites until foamy; gradually add remaining ⅓ cup sugar, beating until stiff peaks form. Fold in chocolate mixture; pour into pie shell. Cover; refrigerate until set, about 4 hours.
8 servings.

Chocolate Surprise Truffles ▲

½ cup unsalted butter, softened
2½ cups confectioners' sugar
½ cup HERSHEY'S Cocoa
¼ cup whipping cream
1½ teaspoons vanilla extract
    Centers: Pecan or walnut
      halves, whole almonds,
      candied cherries, after-
      dinner mints
    Coatings: Confectioners' sugar,
      flaked coconut, chopped nuts

In large mixer bowl cream butter. Combine confectioners' sugar and cocoa; add alternately with whipping cream and vanilla to butter. Blend well. Chill until firm. Shape small amount of mixture around desired center; roll into 1-inch balls. Drop into desired coating and turn until well covered. Chill until firm.
About 3 dozen truffles.

Celebration Chocolate ▶ Frosting

½ cup butter or margarine
¾ cup HERSHEY'S Cocoa
2¾ cups confectioners' sugar
½ cup milk, heated slightly
1 teaspoon vanilla extract
1 egg yolk

In small saucepan over low heat melt butter; add cocoa. Continue to cook, stirring constantly, until smooth. Pour into large mixer bowl; cool. Add confectioners' sugar alternately with milk, beating until smooth and of desired consistency. Blend in vanilla and egg yolk. *About 2¼ cups frosting.*

Celebration Chocolate Cake

¾ cup **HERSHEY'S Cocoa**
1 cup **boiling water**
½ cup **plus 2 tablespoons butter**
    or margarine
2 cups **sugar**
3 **eggs**
1 **teaspoon vanilla extract**
1¾ cups **all-purpose flour**
1½ **teaspoons baking soda**
¼ **teaspoon salt**
¾ **cup milk**
¼ cup **dairy sour cream**
    Celebration Chocolate Frosting
    (recipe page 88)

Heat oven to 350°. Grease three round pans, 9 x 1½ inches. Line bottoms with wax paper; grease and flour paper. In small bowl mix cocoa with boiling water; stir until smooth. Set aside to cool. In large mixer bowl cream butter and sugar until light and fluffy. Add eggs, one at a time, beating well after each addition. Stir in vanilla. Gradually add cocoa mixture; blend well. Combine flour, baking soda and salt; add alternately with milk and sour cream to creamed mixture. Pour into prepared pans. Bake 30 to 35 minutes or until wooden pick inserted in center comes out clean. Cool 10 minutes. Remove from pans; carefully peel off paper. Cool completely. Frost with Celebration Chocolate Frosting. *10 to 12 servings.*

Fudgey Pecan Pie

9-inch unbaked pastry shell
⅓ cup butter or margarine
⅓ cup HERSHEY'S Cocoa
⅔ cup sugar
¼ teaspoon salt
3 eggs, slightly beaten
¾ cup light corn syrup
1 cup chopped pecans (optional)
1 cup pecan halves
   Sweetened whipped cream
      (recipe follows)

Prepare pastry shell; set aside. Heat oven to 375.° In medium saucepan over low heat melt butter; add cocoa and stir until mixture is smooth. Remove from heat; cool slightly. Stir in sugar, salt, eggs and corn syrup; blend thoroughly. Stir in chopped nuts, if desired. Pour into unbaked pastry shell. Place pecan halves over top. Bake 40 minutes. Cool. Cover; let stand about 8 hours before serving. Garnish with sweetened whipped cream. *8 servings.*

Sweetened Whipped Cream: In small mixer bowl combine ½ cup chilled whipping cream, 1 tablespoon confectioners' sugar and ¼ teaspoon vanilla extract; beat until stiff.
About 1 cup topping.

Chocolate Dessert Waffles

½ cup **HERSHEY'S** Cocoa
¼ cup **butter or margarine, melted**
¾ cup **sugar**
 2 **eggs**
 2 **teaspoons vanilla extract**
 1 cup **all-purpose flour**
½ **teaspoon baking soda**
½ **teaspoon salt**
½ cup **buttermilk or sour milk***
½ cup **chopped nuts (optional)**
    Hot Fudge Sauce (recipe page 80)
    Strawberry Dessert Cream
    (recipe follows)

In small mixer bowl blend cocoa and melted butter until smooth; stir in sugar. Add eggs and vanilla; beat well.

Combine flour, baking soda and salt; add alternately with buttermilk to cocoa mixture. Stir in nuts, if desired. Bake in waffle iron according to manufacturer's directions. Carefully remove waffle from iron. Serve warm with Hot Fudge Sauce and Strawberry Dessert Cream. *About ten 4-inch waffles.*

*To sour milk: Use 1½ teaspoons vinegar plus milk to equal ½ cup.

Strawberry Dessert Cream

In small mixer bowl beat 1 cup chilled whipping cream until stiff. Fold in ⅓ cup strawberry preserves and 3 drops red food color, if desired.
About 2 cups topping.

Fun Chocolate Creations

Make good food good fun with these delightful new ways to surprise your friends and family with chocolate.

(Pictured: Chocolate Cream-Filled Choco Tacos, recipe page 102; Chocolate Teddy Bears, recipe page 94; Chocolate Cookie Pretzels, recipe page 95.)

Chocolate Teddy Bears

⅔ cup butter or margarine
1 cup sugar
2 teaspoons vanilla extract
2 eggs
2½ cups all-purpose flour
½ cup HERSHEY'S Cocoa
½ teaspoon baking soda
¼ teaspoon salt

In large mixer bowl cream butter, sugar and vanilla until light and fluffy. Add eggs; blend well. Combine flour, cocoa, baking soda and salt; gradually add to creamed mixture, blending thoroughly. Chill until dough is firm enough to handle. Heat oven to 350°.

To shape teddy bears: For each cookie, form a portion of the dough into 1 large ball for body (1 to 1½ inches), 1 medium-size ball for head (¾ to 1 inch), 4 small balls for arms and legs (½-inch), 2 smaller balls for ears, 1 tiny ball for nose and 4 tiny balls for paws (optional). On ungreased cookie sheet flatten large ball slightly for body. Attach medium-size ball for head by overlapping slightly onto body. Place balls for arms, legs and ears, and a tiny ball on head for nose. Arrange other tiny balls atop ends of legs and arms for paws, if desired. With wooden pick, draw eyes and mouth; pierce small hole at top of cookie for use as hanging ornament, if desired. Bake 6 to 8 minutes or until set. Cool 1 minute on cookie sheet; remove to wire rack. Cool completely. Store in covered container. If cookies will be used as ornaments, allow to dry on wire rack at least 6 hours before hanging. Pull ribbon through hole for hanging.
About 14 cookies.

Chocolate Cookie Pretzels

⅔ cup butter or margarine
1 cup sugar
2 teaspoons vanilla extract
2 eggs
2½ cups all-purpose flour
½ cup HERSHEY'S Cocoa
½ teaspoon baking soda
¼ teaspoon salt
   Confectioners' sugar OR Satiny
   Chocolate Glaze or Peanut
   Butter Chip Frosting
   (optional, recipes follow)

To Make Pretzels: Place strip on un-greased cookie sheet. Twist into pretzel shape by crossing left side of strip to middle, forming loop. Fold right side up and over first loop.

Heat oven to 350° In large mixer bowl cream butter, sugar and vanilla until light and fluffy. Add eggs; blend well. Combine flour, cocoa, baking soda and salt; gradually add to creamed mixture, blending thoroughly. Divide dough into 24 pieces. On lightly floured surface roll each piece with hands into pencil-like strip, about 12 inches long. Place strip on ungreased cookie sheet. Twist into pretzel shape by crossing left side of strip to middle, forming loop. Fold right side up and over first loop. Place about 2 inches apart on cookie sheet. Bake 8 minutes or until set. Cool 1 minute on cookie sheet; remove to wire rack to cool completely. Sprinkle with confectioners' sugar OR frost with Satiny Chocolate Glaze or Peanut Butter Chip Frosting, if desired.
2 dozen cookie pretzels.

Satiny Chocolate Glaze

In small saucepan over low heat melt 2 tablespoons butter or margarine. Add 3 tablespoons HERSHEY'S Cocoa and 2 tablespoons water; stir constantly until mixture thickens. Do not boil. Remove from heat; add ½ teaspoon vanilla extract. Gradually add 1 cup confectioners' sugar, beating with wire whisk until smooth.
About ¾ cup glaze.

Peanut Butter Chip Frosting

Into small mixer bowl measure 1 cup confectioners' sugar; set aside. In small saucepan combine ¼ cup butter or margarine, 3 tablespoons milk and 1 cup REESE'S Peanut Butter Chips. Stir constantly over low heat until chips are melted and mixture is smooth; remove from heat. Add warm mixture to confectioners' sugar; blend in ½ teaspoon vanilla extract. Beat until smooth. Spread while warm.
About 1 cup frosting.

Chocolate-Peanut Butter Coated Apples

10 to 12 wooden skewers
10 to 12 medium apples, stems
    removed
 2 cups (12-ounce package)
    REESE'S Peanut Butter Chips
$\frac{2}{3}$ cup HERSHEY'S Cocoa
$\frac{2}{3}$ cup confectioners' sugar
$\frac{1}{2}$ cup vegetable oil
    Chopped peanuts or flaked
      coconut (optional)

Insert wooden skewer into each washed and thoroughly dried apple. In top of double boiler over hot, not boiling, water combine peanut butter chips, cocoa, confectioners' sugar and oil; stir constantly until chips are melted and mixture is smooth. Remove from heat. Dip apples in mixture; twirl to remove excess coating. (If coating becomes too thick, return to low heat or add additional oil, 1 teaspoon at a time.) Roll lower half of coated apple in peanuts or coconut, if desired. Allow to cool on wax paper-covered tray. Chill, if desired. *10 to 12 apples.*

Chocolate-Marshmallow Turtles

2 cups (12-ounce package)
    HERSHEY'S Semi-Sweet
    Chocolate Chips
2 tablespoons vegetable
    shortening
12 large marshmallows
1½ cups pecan halves

In top of double boiler over hot, not boiling, water molt chocolate chips and shortening, stirring until smooth. Remove from heat. Set aside; cool mixture to 85°F. Cut marshmallows in half horizontally; place on wax paper and flatten slightly. Set aside. On wax paper-covered tray form head and hind feet of turtle by arranging 3 pecan halves with ends touching in center; for front feet, place 1 pecan quarter on each side of head. Arrange 24 of these clusters as bases for turtles. Into center of each cluster of pecans spoon ½ teaspoon melted chocolate mixture. Use fork to dip each marshmallow half in melted mixture to make turtle shell; place each dipped marshmallow over set of pecan clusters, pressing down slightly. Top with pecan half. Cool completely. Store, covered, in refrigerator. *2 dozen snacks.*

Microwave Directions: In 1-quart micro-proof bowl microwave chocolate chips and shortening on high (full power) 1½ to 2 minutes, stirring once, until chips are melted and mixture is smooth when stirred.

Crispy Cocoa Decorations

¼ cup butter or margarine
¼ cup HERSHEY'S Cocoa
5 cups (10½ ounce package)
    miniature marshmallows
5 cups crisp rice cereal
    Decorator Frosting (recipe follows)
    Cinnamon candies, gumdrops,
    colored sprinkles

In large saucepan over low heat melt butter; add cocoa and marshmallows. Cook over low heat, stirring constantly, until marshmallows are melted and mixture is well blended. Continue cooking and stirring 1 minute. Remove from heat. Add cereal; stir until each particle is well-coated. Cool slightly. Butter hands; create shapes such as snowmen, wreaths and trees. If mixture becomes too difficult to mold, return to low heat to soften. Make hole in each ornament for hanging on tree. Cool several hours or overnight. Decorate using Decorator Frosting, cinnamon candies, gumdrops and colored sprinkles. Attach to tree branches.
About 12 ornaments, depending on size and shape.

Ornament Cookies

½ cup butter or margarine
¾ cup sugar
1 egg
¾ teaspoon peppermint extract
1 tablespoon milk
1½ cups all-purpose flour
⅓ cup HERSHEY'S Cocoa
½ teaspoon baking powder
⅛ teaspoon salt
    Decorator Frosting (recipe
    follows)
    Colored sprinkles (optional)

In large mixer bowl cream butter, sugar, egg, peppermint extract and milk until light and fluffy. Combine flour, cocoa, baking powder and salt; add to creamed mixture. Mix until well blended. Divide dough into quarters; wrap tightly. Chill 2 to 3 hours. Heat oven to 325.° On lightly floured surface roll out dough, one quarter at a time, to ⅛-inch thickness. Cut dough with Christmas shaped cookie cutters. Make hole in end of each cookie for hanging on tree. Place cookies 1 inch apart onto ungreased cookie sheet. Bake 8 to 10 minutes or until firm. Cool on wire rack. Decorate using Decorator Frosting and colored sprinkles, if desired.
About 2 dozen cookies.

Decorator Frosting: In small mixer bowl combine 2½ to 3 cups confectioners' sugar, 2 egg whites and ¼ teaspoon peppermint extract. Beat on high speed until stiff. Stir in 1 or 2 drops food color, if desired.

Chocolate Fried Ice Cream

1 quart vanilla ice cream
1 cup vanilla wafer crumbs
1/2 cup finely chopped pecans
1/2 cup flaked coconut
3 tablespoons HERSHEY'S Cocoa
2 eggs
   Vegetable oil
   Chocolate Nut Sauce (recipe
   follows)

With scoop form 6 ice cream balls. Place on wax paper-covered tray; cover and freeze several hours or until very firm. In medium mixing bowl combine vanilla wafer crumbs, pecans, coconut and cocoa; set aside. In small mixing bowl beat eggs. Coat ice cream balls with crumb mixture, pressing crumbs firmly into ice cream. Dip balls in beaten egg; coat again with crumb mixture. Place on wax paper-covered tray; freeze 2 hours or until very firm. Just before serving, heat 2 inches vegetable oil in fry pan or deep fryer to 375.° Remove 2 balls at a time from freezer; fry in hot fat 20 to 25 seconds or until browned. Drain; serve immediately with Chocolate Nut Sauce.
6 servings.

Chocolate Nut Sauce

3 tablespoons butter or margarine
1/3 cup pecan pieces
2/3 cup sugar
1/4 cup HERSHEY'S Cocoa
1/8 teaspoon salt
1/2 cup light cream
1/2 teaspoon vanilla extract

In small saucepan over low heat melt butter; sauté pecans in melted butter until lightly browned. Remove from heat; stir in sugar, cocoa and salt. Add light cream; blend well. Cook over low heat, stirring constantly, until mixture just begins to boil. Remove from heat; add vanilla. Serve warm.
About 1 cup sauce.

"The Best" Chocolate Ice Cream

2 eggs
2 cups sugar, divided
⅔ cup HERSHEY'S Cocoa
2 tablespoons cornstarch
¼ teaspoon salt
2 cups milk
1 tablespoon vanilla extract
4 cups light cream
1 cup whipping cream

In small mixer bowl combine eggs and ½ cup sugar; beat well. In large saucepan combine remaining 1½ cups sugar, cocoa, cornstarch and salt; gradually stir in milk. Cook and stir over medium heat until mixture boils; boil and stir 1 minute. Blend about half of hot mixture into beaten eggs. Stir hot mixture into saucepan. Blend in vanilla, light cream and whipping cream. Chill. Fill ice cream freezer container ⅔ full; freeze according to manufacturer's directions. Remove lid; take out dasher. Pack mixture down; replace lid. Repack in ice and salt. Let stand several hours to ripen. *About 3 quarts ice cream.*

VARIATIONS:

After ice cream is frozen, remove dasher; allow ice cream to ripen one hour. Prepare one of the following additions. Gradually add to partially ripened ice cream, swirling gently to marble. If more firm ice cream is desired, allow additional time to ripen.

Chocolate-Marshmallow: Combine 2 cups marshmallow creme with 2 tablespoons milk. Add as directed above.

Chocolate-Peppermint: Crush hard peppermint candies to equal ¾ cup. Add as directed above.

Chocolate-Peanut Butter: In small saucepan combine 1½ cups REESE'S Peanut Butter Chips, ½ cup sugar and ½ cup milk. Stir over low heat until well blended; cool. Add as directed above.

Chocolate Cream-Filled Choco Tacos

Chocolate Shells

8 taco shells
1¼ cups HERSHEY'S Semi-Sweet
    Chocolate Chips
⅓ cup butter or margarine
1 tablespoon milk
1 cup finely chopped pecans or
    walnuts
8 maraschino cherries (optional)

Heat oven to 350.° Place shells on cookie sheet. Heat 6 minutes; remove from oven. In shallow skillet over very low heat melt chocolate chips and butter, stirring constantly until smooth. Remove from heat. Stir in milk. Place nuts on wax paper-lined tray. Working with one shell at a time, dip entire outer surface in chocolate. Immediately coat outside of shell with nuts. Place coated shells on cool wax paper-covered cookie sheet. Drizzle any remaining chocolate inside shells. Chill 1 to 2 hours or until chocolate hardens. About 2 hours before serving, prepare Chocolate Cream Filling. To serve, fill each shell with about ¼ cup chilled filling. Garnish with reserved whipped cream and maraschino cherry, if desired. *8 servings.*

Chocolate Cream Filling

¾ cup HERSHEY'S Semi-Sweet
    Chocolate Chips
¼ cup milk
½ teaspoon rum extract
½ teaspoon vanilla extract
⅔ cup marshmallow creme
1 cup chilled whipping cream
2 tablespoons confectioners' sugar

In small saucepan combine chocolate chips and milk; cook over low heat, stirring constantly, until chips are melted and mixture is smooth. Remove from heat. Stir in rum extract and vanilla. Pour mixture into large bowl; add marshmallow creme. Whisk until thoroughly blended. Cool. In small chilled mixer bowl beat whipping cream and confectioners' sugar until stiff. Reserve and refrigerate ½ cup whipped cream for garnish. Gently fold remaining whipped cream into chocolate mixture. Cover; place in freezer 1 to 1½ hours to allow flavors to blend.

Recipe courtesy, Mrs. Debbie Yandric, Hershey's THE GREAT AMERICAN CHOCOLATE FESTIVAL® program prize winner, and the Hershey Kitchens.

102

Creamy Cocoa Taffy, Chocolate Mint Patties.

Creamy Cocoa Taffy

1¼ cups sugar
¾ cup light corn syrup
⅓ cup HERSHEY'S Cocoa
⅛ teaspoon salt
2 teaspoons white vinegar
¼ cup evaporated milk
1 tablespoon butter

Butter square pan, 9x9x2 inches; set aside. In heavy 2-quart saucepan combine sugar, corn syrup, cocoa, salt and vinegar. Cook over medium heat, stirring constantly, until mixture boils; add evaporated milk and butter. Continue cooking, stirring occasionally, to 248°F (firm-ball stage) or until syrup, when dropped into very cold water, forms a firm ball that does not flatten when removed from water. Pour mixture into prepared pan. Cool until lukewarm and comfortable to handle. Butter hands; immediately stretch taffy, folding and pulling until light in color and hard to pull. Place taffy on table; pull into ½ inch-wide strips (twist two strips together, if desired). Cut into 1-inch pieces with buttered scissors. Wrap individually. *About 1¼ pounds candy.*

Chocolate Mint Patties

3⅔ cups (1 pound) confectioners' sugar
¼ cup HERSHEY'S Cocoa
⅓ cup butter or margarine
⅓ cup light corn syrup
1 teaspoon peppermint extract
Decorator Frosting (recipe page 99)

Sift together confectioners' sugar and cocoa; set aside. In large mixer bowl on medium speed beat butter, corn syrup and peppermint extract until well blended. Gradually beat in 1 to 2 cups cocoa mixture until well blended and smooth. With wooden spoon stir in remaining cocoa mixture. With hands knead until mixture is well blended and smooth. On wax paper pat or roll out to ¼-inch thickness. With small cookie cutters cut into desired shapes. Decorate using Decorator Frosting. Store in tightly covered container in refrigerator. *About 7 dozen mint patties.*

Filled Rich Chocolate Cupcakes

Filling (recipe follows)
3 cups all-purpose flour
2 cups sugar
⅔ cup HERSHEY'S Cocoa
2 teaspoons baking soda
1 teaspoon salt
2 cups water
⅔ cup vegetable oil
2 tablespoons vinegar
2 teaspoons vanilla extract

Prepare Filling; set aside. Heat oven to 350° In large mixer bowl combine flour, sugar, cocoa, baking soda and salt. Add water, oil, vinegar and vanilla; beat on medium speed 2 minutes or until well combined. Fill paper-lined muffin cups (2½ inches in diameter) ⅔ full with batter. Spoon 1 level tablespoon Filling into center of each cupcake. Bake 20 to 25 minutes or until wooden pick inserted in cake portion comes out clean. Cool. *About 2½ dozen cupcakes.*

Filling

1 package (8 ounces) cream cheese, softened
⅓ cup sugar
1 egg
⅛ teaspoon salt
1 cup HERSHEY'S Semi-Sweet Chocolate Chips or MINI CHIPS

In small mixer bowl combine cream cheese, sugar, egg and salt; beat until smooth and creamy. Stir in chocolate chips.

Goblin's Delight Filling: Add 2 teaspoons grated orange peel, 4 drops yellow food color and 3 drops red food color to Filling before stirring in chips.

Valentine Filling: Add 4 to 5 drops red food color to Filling.

How To Coat Candy

You can make professional-looking candies by using HERSHEY'S "Simple Chocolate Coating." Neither wax nor special "confectioners'" coating is needed with the method.

Making the Centers
Select the recipes for the center you wish to coat and prepare them at least a day ahead. For variety, try different shapes.

Choosing the Right Day
Don't try to make and use coating on a humid day! Humidity, steam or wet equipment cause chocolate to thicken, tighten and become grainy. Even a few drops of water can cause problems. Make sure all utensils are dry before beginning and no water gets into the chocolate mixture while melting.

Assembling the Equipment
Before you begin the coating process, assemble the equipment you need:

- Tape, wax paper and tray.
- Thermometer that registers as low as 100°F.
- Rubber scraper.

- Glass bowl or glass measuring cup to hold the chocolate and shortening.
- Larger glass bowl or a pan to hold the warm water.
- Fondue fork or table fork to dip the centers into coating.

If the instructions are followed *exactly*, glossy chocolate-coated centers will stay firm at room temperature, without "bloom." (Bloom is white or gray spots or streaks that appear when sugar or fat particles separate from chocolate).

The success of this method depends on the very slow melting and constant stirring of the chocolate. With patience and a little practice, you can have professional results.

Helpful Hints
1. Constant scraping and stirring, as stated in the instructions, will help insure success; they are necessary for proper crystal formation.

2. Use solid vegetable shortening as directed, NOT butter, margarine or oil. Butter and margarine contain moisture that can cause chocolate to tighten and become grainy.

In advance, prepare an assortment of centers. Refrigerate until shortly before coating with chocolate.

Bowl containing chocolate must be completely dry. Don't let even one drop of water into mixture.

Chocolate-shortening mixture must be stirred and scraped down constantly with rubber scraper.

Easy Buttercream Centers

1 package (3 ounces) cream
cheese, softened
½ cup butter, softened
4 cups confectioners' sugar
1½ teaspoons vanilla extract

1. In large mixer bowl beat cream cheese and butter until smooth.

2. Blend in confectioners' sugar and vanilla. (If necessary, chill about 1 hour or until mixture is firm enough to handle.)

3. Shape into 1-inch balls; place on wax paper-covered tray.

4. Cover loosely; chill 3 to 4 hours or overnight. Centers should feel dry to touch before coating.

5. Coat centers as directed.
   About 5 dozen centers.

VARIATIONS: Divide mixture into three parts. Add any of the following flavor variations to thirds of the mixture as desired:

⅔ cup flaked coconut
½ teaspoon brandy extract or
   almond extract
½ teaspoon strawberry extract
   plus 3 drops red food color
¼ teaspoon rum extract or orange
   extract
¼ teaspoon mint extract plus 3
   drops green food color

Chocolate Centers: Blend ⅓ cup HERSHEY'S Cocoa with confectioners' sugar and vanilla into above mixture. Add 1 to 2 teaspoons milk until mixture holds together.

Simple Chocolate Coating

2 cups (12-ounce package)
  HERSHEY'S Semi-Sweet
  Chocolate Chips or **MINI CHIPS**
2 tablespoons plus 2 teaspoons
  vegetable shortening (*NOT*
  butter, margarine or oil)

1. Place chocolate and shortening in 4-cup heatproof glass measuring cup or 1½ quart heatproof glass bowl. Fill another larger heatproof glass bowl or large pan with 1 inch of very warm tap water (100°-110°F).

2. Place measuring cup or bowl containing chocolate in the larger bowl or pan so that water covers bottom half of cup or bowl containing chocolate. (Keep water level low so that water does not get into the chocolate mixture and ruin the coating.)

3. Stir CONSTANTLY with rubber scraper until chocolate is completely melted and mixture is smooth. DO NOT RUSH. It will take at least 20 minutes to melt chocolate.

4. If water cools, pour it out and add more warm water (100°-110°F). (Be careful not to get any water into the chocolate mixture.) Remove the measuring cup or bowl containing the melted chocolate mixture from water. Chocolate mixture should be between 84° and 88°F.

5. Dip chilled centers completely into chocolate mixture, one at a time, with fork.

6. Gently tap fork on side of cup or bowl to remove excess chocolate. Invert coated center onto wax paper-covered tray; decorate top of coated center with small amount of melted chocolate, using tip of fork.

7. Store coated centers, loosely covered, in a cool, dry place. *Enough coating for about 5 dozen centers.*

Chocolate mixture should be completely fluid and very smooth before starting to coat centers.

When coating is ready, rest a center on fork; carefully and completely dip into chocolate mixture.

After tapping fork on side of bowl to remove excess coating, invert center onto prepared tray.

Top It Off With Chocolate

Make these delicious frostings, toppings, glazes and syrups for all your special chocolate creations.

(Pictured: Fudge Frosting, recipe page 110; Quick Hot Fudge Sauce, recipe page 110; Chocolate Whipped Cream, recipe page 111.)

Quick Hot Fudge Sauce

2 tablespoons butter or margarine
⅓ cup HERSHEY'S Cocoa
1 can (14 ounces) sweetened
    condensed milk
2 tablespoons water
1 teaspoon vanilla extract

In heavy 2-quart saucepan combine all ingredients except vanilla. Cook over medium heat, stirring constantly with wire whisk, until sauce is smooth and slightly thickened, about 5 minutes. Remove from heat; stir in vanilla. Serve warm over ice cream or desserts. *About 1½ cups sauce.*
sauce.

Microwave Directions: In medium micro-proof bowl microwave butter on high (full power) 30 to 45 seconds or until melted; stir in cocoa until smooth. Blend in sweetened condensed milk and water. Microwave on high 1 minute; stir. Microwave on high 1 to 2 additional minutes, stirring with wire whisk after each minute, or until mixture is smooth and warm. Stir in vanilla. Serve as directed.

◄ Cocoa Glaze

1 cup whipping cream
1 tablespoon light corn syrup
1 cup HERSHEY'S Cocoa
1 cup sugar
2 tablespoons butter
1 tablespoon vanilla extract

In heavy 2-quart saucepan combine cream and corn syrup. Sift cocoa and sugar together; add to cream mixture. Stir well. Add butter. Cook over low heat, stirring constantly, until butter melts and mixture is smooth, about 6 to 8 minutes. Do not boil. Remove from heat; stir in vanilla. Use glaze while warm. *About 2 cups glaze.*

Note: Glaze can be stored in airtight container in refrigerator up to 2 weeks. Reheat over low heat, stirring constantly.

Fudge Frosting

1 cup sugar
¼ cup HERSHEY'S Cocoa
¼ cup butter or margarine
½ cup milk
2 tablespoons light corn syrup
    Dash salt
1½ cups confectioners' sugar
1 teaspoon vanilla extract

In 2-quart saucepan combine sugar and cocoa. Add butter, milk, corn syrup and salt. Bring to full boil over medium heat, stirring constantly. Boil, stirring occasionally, 3 minutes. Remove from heat; cool to lukewarm. In small mixer bowl place confectioners' sugar; stir in chocolate mixture and vanilla. Beat until spreading consistency.
About 2 cups frosting.

Cocoa Cheese Frosting

3 packages (3 ounces each) cream
　　cheese, softened
⅓ cup butter or margarine
5 cups confectioners' sugar
1 cup HERSHEY'S Cocoa
5 to 7 tablespoons light cream

In large mixer bowl blend cream
cheese and butter. Combine confectioners' sugar and cocoa; add alternately with light cream to cream
cheese mixture. Beat until spreading
consistency. *About 3 cups frosting.*

Chocolate Sour Cream Frosting

½ cup butter or margarine
½ cup HERSHEY'S Cocoa
3 cups confectioners' sugar
½ cup dairy sour cream
2 teaspoons vanilla extract

In small saucepan over low heat melt
butter. Add cocoa and stir constantly
until mixture is smooth and slightly
thickened. Transfer to small mixer
bowl; cool slightly. Add confectioners'
sugar alternately with sour cream;
beat to spreading consistency. Stir in
vanilla. *About 2½ cups frosting.*

Sweetened Whipped Cream

1 cup chilled whipping cream
1 to 2 tablespoons confectioners'
　　sugar
½ teaspoon vanilla extract

In small cold mixer bowl combine
cream, confectioners' sugar and
vanilla; beat until stiff. Serve cold.
About 2 cups topping.

Chocolate Whipped Cream: In small
cold mixer bowl combine ½ cup sugar
and ¼ cup HERSHEY'S Cocoa. Add
1 cup chilled whipping cream and 1
teaspoon vanilla extract; beat until
stiff. Serve cold. *About 2 cups topping.*

▼ Fudgey Chocolate Fondue

½ cup butter or margarine
½ cup HERSHEY'S Cocoa
¾ cup sugar
½ cup evaporated milk or light
　　cream
1 teaspoon vanilla extract

In small saucepan over low heat melt
butter. Remove from heat; immediately stir in cocoa. Add sugar and
evaporated milk; cook over low heat,
stirring constantly, until sugar is dissolved and mixture is smooth. Remove
from heat; stir in vanilla. Serve warm
with selection of fruit, marshmallows
or small pieces of cake or cookies.
About 1½ cups fondue.

A Toast To Chocolate

*D*erful beverages made the world over with that special appetite appeal only real chocolate can provide. Cheers!

(Pictured: Irish Cocoa, recipe page 117; Cocoa-Banana Shake, recipe page 115; Hot Cocoa, recipe page 114.)

Hot Cocoa

½ cup sugar
¼ cup HERSHEY'S Cocoa
 Dash salt
⅓ cup hot water
4 cups (1 quart) milk
¾ teaspoon vanilla extract
 Sweetened whipped cream
 (optional)

In medium saucepan combine sugar, cocoa and salt; blend in water. Cook over medium heat, stirring constantly, until mixture boils. Boil and stir 2 minutes. Add milk; stir and heat to serving temperature. DO NOT BOIL. Remove from heat; add vanilla. Beat with rotary beater or wire whisk until foamy. Serve hot, topped with sweetened whipped cream, if desired. *About six 6-ounce servings.*

VARIATIONS:
Add one of the following with vanilla:

Spiced Cocoa: ⅛ teaspoon ground cinnamon and ⅛ teaspoon ground nutmeg.

Citrus Cocoa: ½ teaspoon orange extract or 2 to 3 tablespoons orange liqueur.

Swiss Mocha: 2 to 2½ teaspoons powdered instant coffee.

Mint Cocoa: ½ teaspoon mint extract or 3 tablespoons crushed hard peppermint candy, or 2 to 3 tablespoons white crème de menthe.

Cocoa au lait: Omit whipped cream. Spoon 2 tablespoons softened vanilla ice cream on top of each cup of cocoa at serving time.

Slim-Trim Cocoa: Omit sugar. Combine cocoa, salt and water; substitute skim milk. Proceed as above. With vanilla, stir in sugar substitute with sweetening equivalence of ½ cup sugar.

Microwave Single serving: In microproof cup or mug combine 1 heaping teaspoon HERSHEY'S Cocoa, 2 heaping teaspoons sugar and dash salt. Add 2 teaspoons cold milk; stir until smooth. Fill cup with milk; microwave on high (full power) 1 to 1½ minutes, or until hot. Stir to blend; serve.

Hot Cocoa For a Crowd

1½ cups sugar
1¼ cups HERSHEY'S Cocoa
½ teaspoon salt
¾ cup hot water
4 quarts (1 gallon) milk
1 tablespoon vanilla extract

In 6-quart saucepan combine sugar, cocoa and salt; gradually add hot water. Cook over medium heat, stirring constantly, until mixture boils. Boil and stir 2 minutes. Add milk; heat to serving temperature, stirring occasionally. DO NOT BOIL. Remove from heat; add vanilla. Serve hot. *About twenty-two 6-ounce servings.*

Hot Cocoa Mix

2 cups non-fat dry milk powder
¾ cup sugar
½ cup HERSHEY'S Cocoa
½ cup powdered non-dairy
 creamer
 Dash salt

In large mixing bowl combine all ingredients; blend well. Store in tightly covered container. *3¾ cups mix (about fifteen 6-ounce servings).*

Single Serving: Place ¼ cup mix in heatproof cup or mug; add ¾ cup boiling water. Stir to blend. Serve hot, topped with marshmallow, if desired.

Chocolate Strawberry ▶ Cooler

½ cup sliced strawberries
2 tablespoons sugar
1 tablespoon HERSHEY'S Cocoa
1 cup milk, divided
½ cup club soda, chilled
    Whipped cream or ice cream
2 fresh strawberries (optional)

In blender container combine sliced strawberries, sugar, cocoa and ½ cup milk; cover and blend well. Add remaining ½ cup milk and club soda; cover and blend. Pour into 2 glasses. Garnish with whipped cream or ice cream and strawberry, if desired. Serve immediately.
About two 8-ounce servings.

Mocha Delight

1 cup milk
1 tablespoon HERSHEY'S Cocoa
1 tablespoon sugar
½ teaspoon powdered instant
    coffee
3 to 4 drops almond extract
    (optional)
½ cup vanilla ice cream

In blender container combine milk, cocoa, sugar, instant coffee and almond extract, if desired; cover and blend. Add ice cream; cover and blend until smooth. Serve immediately.
About two 6-ounce servings.

Cocoa-Banana Shake

1 medium-size ripe banana
¼ cup HERSHEY'S Cocoa
¼ cup honey
¼ cup hot water
2 cups cold milk
1 cup vanilla ice cream

Slice banana into blender container. Add cocoa, honey and water; cover and blend until smooth. Add milk; cover and blend. Add ice cream; cover and blend until smooth. Serve immediately. *About four 8-ounce servings.*

Chocolate Egg Nog

4 cups milk, divided
4 eggs, separated
⅓ cup HERSHEY'S Cocoa
1 can (14 ounces) sweetened
    condensed milk
1 teaspoon vanilla extract
¼ teaspoon salt
2 teaspoons brandy extract*
1 teaspoon rum extract*
    Grated chocolate

In blender container combine 1 cup milk, egg yolks, cocoa, sweetened condensed milk, vanilla and salt. Cover and blend on high speed until smooth, about 30 seconds. Pour mixture into large mixing bowl; stir in remaining 3 cups milk and extracts, blending well. Beat egg whites until soft peaks form; gently fold into milk mixture. Refrigerate until well chilled. Stir well before serving. Sprinkle with grated chocolate. *About eight 6-ounce servings.*

*Note: ½ cup brandy or bourbon may be substituted for extracts.

New York Chocolate Egg Cream

¼ cup Cocoa Syrup (recipe follows)
¼ cup light cream
½ cup club soda, freshly opened

All ingredients should be cold. Measure syrup into tall glass; stir in cream to blend. Slowly pour club soda down side of glass, stirring constantly. Serve immediately. *One 8-ounce serving.*

Cocoa Syrup

1½ cups sugar
¾ cup HERSHEY'S Cocoa
Dash salt
1 cup hot water
2 teaspoons vanilla extract

In medium saucepan combine sugar, cocoa and salt. Gradually add water, stirring to keep mixture smooth. Cook over medium heat, stirring constantly until mixture boils; boil and stir 3 minutes. Remove from heat; add vanilla. Pour into heatproof container. Cool; cover and refrigerate. Use as topping for ice cream and desserts, or for chocolate flavored drinks.
About 2 cups syrup.

Hot Merry Mocha

6 tablespoons HERSHEY'S Cocoa
1 to 2 tablespoons powdered
    instant coffee
⅛ teaspoon salt
6 cups hot water
1 can (14 ounces) sweetened
    condensed milk
Sweetened whipped cream
    (optional)

In 4-quart saucepan combine cocoa, instant coffee and salt; stir in water. Cook over medium heat, stirring occasionally, until mixture boils. Stir in sweetened condensed milk; heat thoroughly. DO NOT BOIL. Beat with rotary beater or wire whisk until foamy. Serve hot, topped with sweetened whipped cream, if desired.
About ten 6-ounce servings.

Minted Hot Chocolate: Follow directions above omitting instant coffee. Stir in ¼ to ½ teaspoon mint extract before beating. Serve with candy cane for stirrer, if desired.

Irish Cocoa

6 tablespoons sugar
3 tablespoons HERSHEY'S Cocoa
Dash salt
¼ cup hot water
3 cups milk
6 tablespoons Irish whiskey
½ cup chilled whipping cream,
    whipped

In medium saucepan combine sugar, cocoa and salt; stir in water. Cook over medium heat, stirring constantly, until mixture boils. Boil and stir 2 minutes. Add milk; stir and heat to serving temperature. DO NOT BOIL. Remove from heat. Pour 1 tablespoon whiskey in each cup or goblet. Fill cup with hot cocoa; stir to blend. Serve hot, topped with whipped cream.
About six 6-ounce servings.

The Finishing Touch

__T__hese creative garnishes add a special touch to your favorite chocolate desserts.

Chocolate Party Cups

**2 cups (12-ounce package)
HERSHEY'S Semi-Sweet
Chocolate Chips
2 teaspoons vegetable shortening
(not butter, margarine or oil)**

In top of double boiler over hot, not boiling, water melt chips and shortening, stirring until smooth; remove from heat. Cool slightly. In muffin pans place twelve paper or foil baking cups (2½ inches in diameter). Using a narrow, soft-bristled pastry brush, thickly and evenly coat inside pleated surface and bottom of each cup. Chill coated cups 10 minutes or until set; coat any thin spots again. (If necessary, chocolate mixture may be reheated over hot water.) Cover tightly; chill until very firm, about 1 hour. Carefully peel paper from each cup. Cover and chill at least 1 hour. Fill chilled cups as desired.
About 12 dessert cups.

Chocolate Butterflies

In top of double boiler over hot, not boiling, water melt 1 cup HERSHEY'S Semi-Sweet Chocolate Chips; stir until completely melted. Cool slightly. Into small pastry bag fitted with a writing tip or into parchment bag spoon melted chocolate. On wax paper pipe chocolate in a steady flow into butterfly shape. Fold small, narrow strip of double-thickness aluminum foil into "M" shape. Gently place butterfly on wax paper into center of the "M," allowing wings to rest against sloped sides. Pipe strip of melted chocolate into the center of the "M" to reinforce butterfly body. Cover; chill until shapes are firm. Remove butterflies from refrigerator; carefully peel wax paper away from chocolate. Place on tray; cover and refrigerate until ready to use.

Chocolate Triangles and Wedges

In top of double boiler over hot, not boiling, water melt 1 cup HERSHEY'S Semi-Sweet Chocolate Chips; stir until completely melted. On wax paper-covered cookie sheet spread melted chocolate with spatula into 8-inch square or circle. Chill 5 to 8 minutes or just until chocolate begins to set.

With sharp knife score chocolate square into smaller squares; cut each small square diagonally in half to make triangles. Score chocolate circle into pie-like wedges. Do not try to separate at this time. Cover; chill several hours or until very firm. Carefully peel wax paper away from chocolate; gently separate triangles or wedges at score marks. Place on tray; cover and refrigerate until ready to use.

Chocolate Leaves

Thoroughly wash and dry leaves to be coated. In top of double boiler over hot, not boiling, water melt ⅔ cup HERSHEY'S Semi-Sweet Chocolate Chips; stir until completely melted. With small soft-bristled pastry brush, brush melted chocolate on top of each leaf. (Use underside of leaf for more distinct vein markings.) Avoid getting chocolate on other side of leaf or removal may be difficult. Place on wax paper-covered cookie sheet; chill until very firm. Carefully peel or tear leaves away from chocolate. Place on tray; cover and refrigerate until ready to use.

Note: Many leaves are safe for coating; check with florist if in doubt.

Chocolate Curls

The secret to successful curls is chocolate at the proper temperature, slightly warm but still firm. On a warm day, room temperature might be fine.

Place unwrapped HERSHEY'S Milk Chocolate Bar, SPECIAL DARK Bar, or Unsweetened Baking Chocolate on cookie sheet. Place in cooled oven until warm. (Or place in microwave oven on high power about 30 seconds or just until chocolate feels slightly warm.) With even pressure draw vegetable peeler along underside of chocolate; a curl will form. Use wooden pick to lift curl onto wax paper-covered tray. Refrigerate until firm.

Use side of candy bar for narrow curls. Use width of one or two blocks for medium-size curls. Use entire width of bar for large curls.

Note: Chocolate curls can be refrigerated in covered container and stored for later use.

Index

G

H

I

J

M

Here's How to Make It Chocolate with HERSHEY'S

SEND a check or money order for $3.95 plus two (2) proofs of purchase from any combination of these products:

HERSHEY'S COCOA—cash register receipt with price circled

HERSHEY'S CHOCOLATE CHIPS—UPC symbol from 11.5 oz., 12 oz., or 24 oz. bags

HERSHEY'S BAKING CHOCOLATE—UPC symbol

REESE'S. NATURALLY FLAVORED PEANUT BUTTER CHIPS—UPC symbol

Mail your check or money order with your name, address, city, state and zip on a 3" x 5" card to:

"MAKE IT CHOCOLATE," P.O. Box 8089-C, Ronks, PA 17573

Allow 8 weeks for delivery. Offer void where prohibited. Valid only in U.S.A.